GOD'S CONSTANT PRESENCE
True Stories of Everyday Miracles

Lifted
by His Word

GOD'S CONSTANT PRESENCE

True Stories of Everyday Miracles

Lifted *by* His Word

EDITORS OF GUIDEPOSTS

A Gift from Guideposts

Thank you for your purchase! We appreciate your support and want to express our gratitude with a special gift just for you.

Dive into **Spirit Lifters**, a complimentary booklet that will fortify your faith and offer solace during challenging moments. It contains 31 carefully selected verses from scripture that will soothe your soul and uplift your spirit.

Please use the
QR code or go to
guideposts.org/spiritlifters
to download.

Lifted by His Word

Published by Guideposts
100 Reserve Road, Suite E200
Danbury, CT 06810
Guideposts.org

Cover design by Serena Fox Design Company
Interior design by Serena Fox Design Company
Cover photo © Shutterstock: Eran Porat
Typeset by Aptara, Inc.

ISBN 978-1-961441-21-7 (hardcover)
ISBN 978-1-961441-22-4 (softcover)
ISBN 978-1-961441-23-1 (epub)

Printed and bound in the United States of America

The secret things belong to the LORD our God, but the things revealed belong to us and to our children forever, that we may follow all the words of this law.

—*Deuteronomy 29:29 (NIV)*

situation and everyday events, whereas our "actual life" is the flow beneath those things.

I can relate to this idea of two simultaneous lives. I have my very busy day-to-day as a full-time pastor and mother. I wake up early, get kids off to school, get to the church for a full day of writing and visits, then head home to juggle the schedule of making dinner and taking kids to evening activities, then going to bed late—simply to wake up tomorrow and do it all again. But underneath that is my actual life, or what really matters. The things I think about God and the world. My personal struggles with pain and disappointment. The relationships I am trying to nurture with my husband and my children. That is my actual life; those are the things that really matter.

In Jacob's story, he is jolted out of the busy life and into his actual life—and it is there that he finds God. It is there that he discovers what really matters, and the course of his life is changed.

Finding our way out of the busyness of life can be a real struggle. For me, a focus on devotional time and reading the Bible is often what draws me closer to God. It helps me to slow down, to plug in, and to find that deeper true life that Rohr talks about.

My absolute favorite scripture that I go to for hope and comfort is Psalm 46 (quoted here in the NIV):

> God is our refuge and strength,
> an ever-present help in trouble.
> Therefore we will not fear, though the earth give way
> and the mountains fall into the heart of the sea,
> though its waters roar and foam
> and the mountains quake with their surging.
> There is a river whose streams make glad the city of God,
> the holy place where the Most High dwells.

God is within her, she will not fall;
   God will help her at break of day.
Nations are in uproar, kingdoms fall;
   he lifts his voice, the earth melts.
The LORD Almighty is with us;
   the God of Jacob is our fortress.
Come and see what the LORD has done,
   the desolations he has brought on the earth.
He makes wars cease
   to the ends of the earth.
He breaks the bow and shatters the spear;
   he burns the shields with fire.
He says, "Be still, and know that I am God;
   I will be exalted among the nations,
   I will be exalted in the earth."
The LORD Almighty is with us;
   the God of Jacob is our fortress.

The psalmist paints a picture of the world falling apart. Chaos reigns in both the natural world and the physical world, but God has power over all these forces. Even when the earth shakes and floods rise, even when the nations are in an uproar, God is in control.

It is into this unrest that the psalmist tells us to behold the desolations of God. We might expect a story about God destroying all the people, as we so often find in the Old Testament. But surprisingly, here God only destroys the weapons of war. Bow, spear, and shield are all thrown down and shattered as God declares, "Be still!"

I think that this is a call for people to stop their maddening ways. Just as we might yell at our kids to stop fighting or raise our voice to get control over a fidgety classroom, God calls out, "Be still, and know that I am God; I will be exalted among the nations, I will be exalted in the earth." *Knock it off and be still!* If only we could slow down and connect with God the way God longs for us to do.

"God is our refuge and strength, an ever-present help in trouble." The psalmist encourages us to seek God as a place of safety in a frightening world. God is not a refuge *from* the world; rather, God is a refuge *within* the world. And when we take the time to connect with God through devotion and prayer, we find the refuge that our hearts so desire.

More than anything, I think we long to feel an assurance of God's presence in our midst. We want to see God. We want to know God. We want to have an encounter with the holy.

When Moses was leading the Israelites out of Egypt, he too felt this desire. While he was on the mountaintop receiving the Ten Commandments, the people down below were fashioning a golden calf. When Moses returned to the people, both he and God were beyond angry. God said that He didn't want to go with the people into the Promised Land anymore. Their faithlessness was driving Him away.

> For the LORD had said to Moses, "Tell the Israelites, 'You are a stiff-necked people. If I were to go with you even for a moment, I might destroy you. Now take off your ornaments and I will decide what to do with you.'"
> (Exodus 33:5, NIV)

Moses boldly approaches God again on the mountaintop and begs God to go with him and the people. Moses doesn't want to go alone, Moses doesn't want to lead alone, and Moses knows that an angel will not be enough to convince the people that they have the blessing of God. They need the very presence of God in their midst if they are going to have the courage to face the wilderness.

When God finally agrees to go, Moses asks for something more: "Show me your glory." Like us, Moses wants to see God. And not just the person of God, or the face of God. Moses wants to see the goodness and glory of God. Surprisingly, God agrees: "I will cause all my goodness to pass in front of you, and I will proclaim my name, the LORD, in your presence" (Exodus 33:19, NIV).

But God is too scary and awesome to be fully seen by humanity.

> "But," he said, "you cannot see my face, for no one may see me and live." Then the LORD said, "There is a place near me where you may stand on a rock. When my glory passes by, I will put you in a cleft in the rock and cover you with my hand until I have passed by. Then I will remove my hand and you will see my back; but my face must not be seen." (Exodus 33:20–23, NIV)

And so we have this touching story of a bodily God hiding Moses in the cleft of a rock, passing by and covering Moses with His hand, and then finally removing the covering so that Moses can see the back of God as He walks away. It's a wonderfully tender image.

I see such a connection between Moses's experience and our own. Moses wants assurance that God is with him. He wants certainty. And we want that too.

We want to know that God goes with us as we venture out into the wilderness of our own lives. I believe that, like Jacob and Moses, we still have glimpses of the divine: When we feel a baby kick through her mother's tummy. When we hold our own child for the first time, and we feel like our heart could either burst or break. When we hear a perfect performance of live music and for some reason all the hair on the back of our neck stands up. Or when we smell something that suddenly transports us back to another time and place. All of these things are glimpses of God, all of these things are God's presence in our lives. All of these assurances of God's presence are available to us, if we just keep looking for them, if we just keep connecting to the story of God.

Moses longs for God to go with him into life. Moses longs to see God fully, and he doesn't get that, but he does catch a glimpse of God walking by. So, too, we have those moments that make us believe that life is something more. In my own life, I am thinking of the times my church celebrates communion at a nursing home. For some reason, God always shows up there. I don't know why it's that place or those times, but when I play the piano and we pass the bread and juice, I can feel in my heart that there's a presence in the room with us. It is often when we are sharing or being in ministry together that we catch these glimpses. At the communion table, singing a hymn, in the moment of silent prayer, visiting a friend in the hospital, reading our Bibles—those are the times when we feel God.

Kids are the best at showing us the way. I will never forget the time my four-year-old daughter, Olivia, drew a nativity picture on one of those magnetic wipe boards kids play with. It was a complete scene, with Mary and Joseph and the baby in a box with all of these fuzzy sheep. And in the sky was a fuzzy black shape. I pointed to it. "What is that?" I asked, thinking it was a cloud. "Jesus is dreaming about petting the black sheep,"

Olivia said to me, as if the answer was obvious. You could have knocked me over with a feather. How did my baby come up with something so profound? She has no idea what it means to be a black sheep, or that Jesus favors the outsider. Kids are unfiltered and they have an innate connection with the divine.

But we get old, and our days are long, and like the Israelites, we get distracted by sparkly things. We forget about drawings and dreams and Jesus. We forget about God and brushes with the divine. And it takes more to wake us from sleep. We know something is missing, but we don't know what it is. And so we find ourselves reading a devotional from Guideposts, or a collection of true stories, like this one, where others share their own glimpses of God. We are seeking, looking, and longing for more.

How do we know God goes with us? Because that is the promise of our faith. That is the promise of God's Word. We are never alone when we have the stories of Scripture to guide us.

My friends, may God go with you and bless you as you read this book today. Amen.

———◆———

God meets daily needs
daily. Not weekly or
annually. He will give
you what you need when
it is needed.

—Max Lucado

CHAPTER 1

A Verse at the Right Moment

Love Never Fails

Lisa Saruga

How on earth did we get here, Lord? My two preteen sons were
asleep in their rooms, and I lay awake in my bedroom alone—
again. I prayed that my boys would be unscarred by the
divorce. Having experienced my parents' divorce when I was
a teen, I wanted to protect them from the pain and uncertainty
I'd known.

I had been married to their father for a complicated 10 years,
and we had spent 7 of those years in counseling. I wanted God
to heal our marriage and our family, so I was willing to put
every effort into learning how we could work together as a
team. When my first husband remarried only 2 weeks after our
divorce was final, I felt anew the sting of rejection.

Two years later, I remarried. This man was from a Christian
family. I was certain God had blessed me with a second chance.
Now I was alone for a second time. When my second husband moved out to pursue another relationship, I was shocked,
devastated, and mortified. I now lived with the emotional scars
and shame. This shame didn't stem from anything I had done
wrong; it was the fear of how others would view me. Who
would take a twice-divorced woman seriously when she shared
the good news of the love and power of God?

I could identify with the woman at the well from John
chapter 4. Jesus had known she had been married multiple

times and was living with a man who was not her husband. That woman had been shunned, not only by the men in her life, but by her entire community. She lived with shame and hid from others who disapproved of her lifestyle.

What was the rest of her story? Had she been wild and impulsive, or had she been rejected time and again? Was she a sinner, or was she a victim? She was perceived to be a sinner, and yet, God had used her to spread the news of Jesus.

Could I ever be a credible witness again, or would others doubt my faith and character? I knew my faith in God had been unshaken, but I had to remind myself that I was not responsible for the decisions of my ex-husbands. It would have been easy to question what I had done wrong to deserve their rejection.

> **Love is patient, love is kind. It does not envy, it does not boast, it is not proud.**
>
> —1 CORINTHIANS 13:4 (NIV)

Following my second divorce, I started a ministry at my church called Single Purpose. I wanted to demonstrate that it is possible to live a happy, productive life serving the Lord as a single person. I made it clear I would not date any members of this singles group. It was an easy promise, because I didn't plan to date or marry again.

My boys had grieved when their father moved out, and grieved a second time when they lost their stepfather. I would never set them—or me—up for that kind of loss again.

As I lay in my bed praying for my boys, loneliness overwhelmed me. Staying single was an easy way to avoid further pain, but I longed for a companion to navigate life with.

I began to write a letter to God in my journal. As I shared my lonely thoughts, I also "informed" God that I couldn't allow another man into my life. How could I trust myself to choose a faithful life partner?

"Lord, if you ever want me to date again, You will have to choose the man for me. This is my list of nonnegotiables." I filled a page with things that would make a man eligible for my attention. He had to be a devoted Christian, one who loves music and practices self-control. The list was long, but I topped my list with this admittedly curious expectation: "He has to have memorized 1 Corinthians 13:4–8."

The next week, after a time of praise and worship, our Single Purpose group began a lively, fast-paced icebreaker game. A man I hadn't seen before introduced himself.

"Hi. My name is Barry. I'm checking out this ministry because I lead a divorce recovery group at another church. I think some of my people might benefit from joining your group."

Several people had asked if I knew him because of our adjacent ministries. Although we had lived in the same small town for many years, we had never met. During our icebreaker game, he was gregarious and funny. Although it wasn't the purpose of our group to matchmake, it crossed my mind that some of the women might find him a breath of fresh air.

At the end of the night, I was surprised when Barry said, "I understand that you don't date anyone from this group, so I won't be returning. Would you like to go for a walk with me tomorrow?"

Caught off-guard, I thought of my note to God. *How will I know if my nonnegotiables are met if I never take a risk?* A walk sounded harmless enough. We agreed to meet at a local park a few days later.

It was a beautiful evening, and talk flowed easily. At one point, Barry began humming an old hymn. It seemed natural and comfortable, so I began to sing along. We broke into harmony and praised the name of Jesus as we walked.

Wasn't a love of music on my list of nonnegotiables?

As the song came to an end, Barry, unprompted, began to quote the very verses from 1 Corinthians that I'd listed in my journal: "Love is patient, love is kind. It does not envy, it does not boast, it is not proud. It does not dishonor others, it is not self-seeking, it is not easily angered, it keeps no record of wrongs. Love does not delight in evil but rejoices with the truth. It always protects, always trusts, always hopes, always perseveres. Love never fails."

> **I will be glad and rejoice in your love, for you saw my affliction and knew the anguish of my soul.**
>
> —PSALM 31:7 (NIV)

Now God had my attention! He was clearly showing me that Barry was safe. I agreed to a second walk, and then to a motorcycle ride. His marriage had ended when his wife had been unfaithful, so he understood my pain and regret. When I shared that I had been twice divorced, he had questions, but he never judged me or suggested that it was my fault.

Barry was a man of his word. He never returned to Single Purpose. Both of us were cautious and careful. He, too, had a list of nonnegotiables. Trust wasn't instant between us, so we agreed to interview each other's friends and coworkers. We interrogated each other over shared dinners. We even signed releases to talk to each other's therapists, just to be certain neither of us were psychopaths on a mission to cause further pain.

After a few months of investigating each other, I asked, "Can we just spend time together and get to know one another? I think we might actually enjoy each other's company."

Barry laughed, and we agreed to let down our emotional guards. Over time, we introduced our children and allowed them to spend time together. Slowly it dawned on me that God had introduced me to a man who met *every* expectation on my list of nonnegotiables.

Barry had not only memorized 1 Corinthians 13:4–8; he was the embodiment of those verses. He *was* patient and kind. He never dishonored me. I could trust that he was not so self-seeking that he would pursue other women as he professed his love for me. Barry demonstrated that his love for Jesus—his drive to be of good character for the sake of his faith—was greater than his love even for me.

Barry and I recently celebrated our twentieth wedding anniversary. God chose wisely. Love never fails.

The Great "I AM"

Roberta Messner

Most folks come to Sarka-Kauffmann Jewelers, the premiere jew-elry store in Huntingdon, West Virginia, to leave with something lasting. I was here to relinquish it. As I elbowed open the heavy plate glass door, my eyes took in the sign that read "Diamonds Are Forever," then moved to the diamond-studded tennis bracelet in my plastic sandwich bag. A gift to myself on my thirtieth birthday. For over three decades, that bracelet had been a sparkling constant in my life. I'd worn it to special events, to church, to my job as a nurse, and even around my old log cabin in a pair of jeans.

Now, the doctors had found a new tumor, another in the long line of painful tumors that had plagued me since I was a little girl. I had a big surgery ahead. An insurance copay even bigger. *You can't wear a diamond tennis bracelet to the OR, Roberta.* Kelly, the owner of the store, looked at me with understanding eyes as she took the Ziploc baggie. She'd been with me through it all. Knew I had an eye for things that shine; there just wasn't much shining in my pocket anymore.

Diamond prices had been on the upturn, and Kelly had phoned. Passing her the bracelet was like handing over hope. One tumor, one medical complication, one new prescription after another. Insurance simply didn't cover everything. I'd gone through my hard-earned savings. Exchanged dear keepsakes for short-lived promises of good health.

I was still missing that bracelet on my wrist when Kelly called a few days later. "I've been going through the scrap jewelry here at the store," she said. Her mention of the word *scrap* sent a shiver through my spine. Kelly had known me through my descent into agonizing tumor pain, addiction to prescription opioids, medical debt, and hopelessness. I wasn't sure she knew about my fear of ending up in the scrap heap myself.

But there was something in her voice. Kindness—a hand reaching from her fancy jewelry store on Huntington's Fourth Avenue to me in my old log cabin on Aracoma Road. I listened closely. "Between what *you* have, Roberta, and *my* stash, I think we could have a lot of fun."

God said to Moses, "I AM WHO I AM."

—EXODUS 3:14 (NIV)

Fun in the middle of this nightmare? It seemed impossible, but Kelly was undeterred. I didn't exactly know why, but for the first time in months, I felt something akin to excitement. After a doctor's appointment, I stopped in to see her. Before I knew what was happening, silver-toned hearts and other charms shimmered on the glass countertop.

In my own discards, I had found a sturdy silver chain that held them all just so, including a filigree cross that Kelly placed among the array of hearts. When I wore the charm necklace to work the following day, my coworkers asked about it. I told them about crafting it with Kelly, who'd encouraged me with every addition to that chain. How each heart, different in design, had reminded me of one more thing I'd gotten through.

"I love it!" a fellow nurse said. "Jewelry that tells a story. You've had some pretties in your time, Roberta, but nothing quite like this."

Throughout the workday, I'd find myself fingering those little hearts, remembering the love that had been there for me. The silver cross in the center—too long relegated to a dusty jewelry box—spoke of the greatest love of all.

A few days later, I boarded an elevator to make rounds on the oncology ward. A patient's wife with tired eyes told me her husband's cancer was back. I felt a tug in my spirit. She needed the story more than I did. When I clasped the necklace around her neck, as Kelly had done on mine, joy bubbled inside me that no diamond could rival.

Kelly and I cobbled together one necklace after another. Our creations found their way to strangers who marveled that a cross and a clown might reside side by side on a chain—or in a life. Scraps of jewelry nobody wanted made a one-of-a-kind statement on one neck after another. Folks telling their stories. I got to hear their stories; they had different troubles than I, different lives. But we had one thing in common: the God who sees it all and sees us through.

One morning at the hospital, I noticed a lady exchanging a quarter for a bag of popcorn the hospital volunteers were selling. When she saw my necklace, she smiled as if it held a divine secret. I knew that it had been waiting for her all along.

When I clasped it around the jewel neck of her black sweater, she caressed its charms, then held onto the two-toned,

> **Let your adorning be the hidden person of the heart with the imperishable beauty of a gentle and quiet spirit, which in God's sight is very precious.**
>
> —1 PETER 3:4 (ESV)

silver-and-gold cross for dear life. "I don't even know you," she said. "But this necklace is telling my story. Yours too. In God's hands, there's always a new chapter." She passed the popcorn to her wheelchair-bound husband. The elevator door opened. And just like that, she was gone.

But not her words. I didn't know it then, but I was firmly in God's hands, and there was a new chapter coming for me too.

On Easter Sunday morning in 2018, I was miraculously healed of a lifetime of tumor pain and addiction to prescription opioids. When the news reached Kelly, she asked me to come to Sarka-Kauffmann Jewelers. As in days past, I elbowed open the heavy plate glass door.

> **A word fitly spoken is like apples of gold in a setting of silver.**
>
> —PROVERBS 25:11 (ESV)

Waiting on the glass counter, against a backdrop of black velvet, was a two-sided sterling silver pendant Kelly had designed from vintage cast-offs—old charms, rhinestone buttons from a grandma's dress, and other objects time had forgotten. On one side were hand-cuffs, symbolizing the shackles of pain and addiction that were no more. Beside them she'd engraved the words, "I WAS." On the reverse, an open Bible and the words, "I AM." She'd made me a lasting reminder of the day everything changed because of The Great I AM.

Then something happened that was so amazing that it stuns me still.

On a long road trip, dressed in total grunge, I stopped at a bookstore in Lexington, Kentucky, to break up my trip. While I was thumbing through a volume in the store's Lifestyle

GOD'S GIFT OF TOUCH
— Eryn Lynum —

RUNNING A FINGER over a felled tree stump, one can feel the slight grooves of its inner rings. This is a way to count the tree's years of life and read its story. Narrow rings reflect seasons of drought and limited growth. Wide rings tell of plentiful years with abundant rain and maturation. Abrupt marks and scars are punctuations of tragedy or adversity, such as wildfire or a lightning strike. Following marks of hardship, one can often notice years of healthy growth after. This is also how God works in the lives of His children. Challenges and even calamities are not the end of a story, but rather a significant turning point from which growth often follows.

section, a distinguished doctor and author who had been signing copies of her latest release left her table and tapped me on the shoulder.

"I couldn't help noticing you when you walked in," she said. "Could I tell you something?"

I nodded.

"The moment I saw you, God spoke to my spirit. He has a new life for you. He wants you to live the promise of The Great I AM."

How had she known? I had left Kelly's pendant in my car. I went out to retrieve it, to share the great love and care of our Lord.

A look of peaceful assurance came over the author's face when she saw the necklace. Shoppers circled at her table as I shared my story. The author's daughter captured the moment in a photograph, the esteemed doctor dressed in book-signing finery, and me in a scruffy flannel shirt, holding Kelly's pendant close to my heart.

These days, I mostly wear the pendant side that declares, "I AM." But on days I need a reminder, the words "I WAS" take center stage. The handcuffs tell the story of a girl imprisoned by a lifetime of pain and everything that goes with it.

All of our stories are different, yet not one of us escapes some form of pain. When I share my story with others, I love to tell them how they, too, can know The Great I AM. I tell them about Kelly's creation, born in the scrap heap. And of the God beyond all imaginings, who gave me not diamonds, but something that really is forever: A new life and the jewelry to prove it.

Not unto Death

A. J. Larry

My husband, John, and I host a Bible study and prayer line with a group of twelve God-loving individuals. Every Wednesday evening, we gather on a dedicated phone line to pray over our ever-growing prayer list and share in God's Word. Participants call in from different states, but when we join for prayer and Bible study, it feels as though we are unified in one place. Each week, one person leads the group in the opening prayer and shares an encouraging word from Scripture. After reading and discussing the passages, others chime in, sharing how those verses have touched their hearts. Sometimes as we encourage one another, God's Word speaks quietly, yet pointedly and unexpectedly, to our individual hearts.

In late July of 2021, on a Tuesday evening, my stomach felt delicate, so I opted for a light meal and warm liquids to soothe it. By Wednesday, I had developed a congested cough and debated whether I should participate in the conference call. After brief consideration, I decided that a minor cough was manageable. However, during the call, I excused myself multiple times to clear my throat and found it challenging to maintain focus during the prayer and Scripture reading.

The scriptures for that night were from John chapter 10, but my eyes trailed over to John 11:4 (NKJV), which says: "This sickness is not unto death." Although that verse was not a part of our study, it gripped my spirit and clung to my heart tenaciously. I tried shaking it off by redirecting my thoughts back to our Bible study, convinced that John 11:4 wasn't meant for me in that moment. In my mind, a little cough and an upset stomach did not constitute sickness. However, as I rejoined our Bible study, John 11:4 persisted, refusing to release its hold on me.

Later that night, as I lay in bed, I engaged in prayer, pondering the relevance of the scripture to my situation. I wondered if perhaps the verse had been intended for me to intercede on behalf of someone else who might be unwell. I thought long and hard about family members and friends who were struggling with their health and prayed for them. However, just a couple days later, I found myself bedridden and helpless with Covid-19.

> **When Jesus heard that, He said, "This sickness is not unto death, but for the glory of God, that the Son of God may be glorified through it."**
>
> **—JOHN 11:4 (NKJV)**

Despite immediate quarantine, Covid-19 swept through our home like a whirlwind. Over the course of a week, John—the last man standing in a household of three women (myself, our eldest daughter, Sharina, and eldest granddaughter, Kiera)—took charge of cooking, serving, cleaning, and sanitizing before Covid-19 gradually took him down. Each of us experienced a range of symptoms: excessive coughing, headaches, chills, fever, shortness of breath, difficulty breathing, loss of smell and taste, and loss of appetite. We all bore the weight of extreme muscle weakness and fatigue. We sent texts to family members to inform them of our state, and my siblings graciously dropped off items to aid in our recovery.

I was overcome with worry when I learned that our youngest daughter's household (except for her 14-year-old son, who miraculously escaped it) was also battling Covid-19. To make matters worse, John, our youngest granddaughter, Kamarie, and I all had preexisting conditions that made the virus more dangerous for us. Kamarie had struggled with bladder and kidney issues since childhood, so my heart ached for her safety.

As we fought to survive, I realized the reason that my attention had been drawn so strongly to John 11:4—God's Word was meant not only for me but for my family as well.

Covid-19 made death feel imminent and sudden. Perhaps the breathing problems evoked memories of a time I had been critically ill and struggling to

You will keep him in perfect peace, whose mind is stayed on You, because he trusts in You.

—ISAIAH 26:3 (NKJV)

breathe at 17. My life seemed to be slipping away slowly then, as it seemed to be again now. Determined not to succumb to Covid-19, I drew in the deepest breath I could muster. On the exhale, I recited John 11:4 with all my might: "This sickness is not unto death." I wanted to affirm that God had directed me to His Word on that evening in late July before I even knew I was ill, and remind myself that I trusted that He would hear my feeble cry and come to my aid.

When it felt as though the virus had depleted me of every ounce of energy I had left, I found myself, against my will, in the emergency room amongst other Covid-19 patients. With no family by my side—visitors were not allowed for fear of spreading the virus—I struggled to keep up with the attendant who led me to a makeshift private area. There, I witnessed other patients, moving like zombies, awaiting confirmation of their diagnosis. It was a heartbreaking sight, especially knowing how many had already succumbed to Covid-19.

> **He welcomed them and spoke to them about the kingdom of God, and healed those who needed healing.**
>
> —LUKE 9:11 (NIV)

The hospital was near full; only a few beds were available for admission. Prior to Covid-19, I had been scheduled for an iron infusion due to an anemia-related deficiency. Now that I was at the hospital, I hoped I could receive the infusion as well as treatment for my breathing issues and then return home. Instead, doctors ran tests and called in prescriptions to a pharmacy, then released me to return home.

My anxiety rose, because I wasn't able to get the breathing inhaler I needed until two days later, but the word of the Lord remained rich in my spirit: "This sickness is not unto death." And He provided. Just in time, a gift arrived from my sister, a Himalayan salt inhaler that helped to ease my breathing until the prescriptions could be filled.

Sharina and Kiera recovered first after three weeks with the virus and then began to help members of our family. Kiera was, thankfully, able to remain home with John and me, while Sharina went to her sister's home to help take care of their family, including my grandson, who had been managing alone. My heart was relieved when she reported that everyone was well. I knew God was being faithful to His Word.

Over the 8 weeks that the virus lingered in John and me, extreme muscle weakness and fatigue continued to plague us. Our appetites remained minimal as the virus wreaked havoc on our taste and smell. Still, I clung to John 11:4 as if it were oxygen required for breathing. Finally, complete healing took place.

Though we later speculated about it, none of us knew how Covid-19 had entered our homes. However, it prompted us to reflect on the true value of time, health, and life. Most importantly, we praised God for complete healing and His infinite Word and mercy—and especially for the reassuring words that He sent me to sustain me throughout my sickness.

Led to Psalm 16

Stacey Thureen

It was a typical Wednesday morning. After I completed my morning devotions and prayer time, I made my way downstairs to start the day's laundry. I could hear my oldest two children, Avery and Dane, talking in the kitchen as they made their breakfast.

There are some mornings when I wake up and sense peace in the home. Other mornings, I can feel tension brewing like a strong pot of coffee that's about to spill over. Often, when I sense the stress, I find myself praying out loud somewhere between the entrance to our upstairs bedroom and the hallway to the kitchen. That morning, I prayed out loud: "Lord, I pray for peace and protection over our home. In Jesus's name. Amen."

But by the time I had finished loading the washer and packing a few things my preschooler, Joy, would need for her day, I could hear that Avery and Dane's conversation had turned into strong sibling dialogue. I walked into the kitchen and found them arguing over who would get the last packet of strawberries and cream oatmeal. I persuaded them to share and thought, *Phew, one small crisis averted.*

Unfortunately, another one was on the way. Suddenly, I heard Joy screaming and crying so loudly that it hurt my ears. I raced as fast as I could up the stairs to her bedroom. There she was, sitting upright in her new big-girl bed. Wailing with tears, Joy placed her hand on her right ear. "Joy, does your ear hurt?"

With tears streaming down her face, she nodded her head yes. I quickly grabbed a thermometer from the master bedroom's bathroom and took her temperature. She had a fever.

All that was ahead for the day flashed through my mind. I was training for an upcoming masters swim meet and needed to work out at our local YMCA. While the dryland and weight machine equipment were better there, I knew that I could do a lot of those exercises at home if needed. *God, thank You this happened on a day when I can shift gears and adjust a little bit.*

But then there was the dreaded notion of having to take Joy to see the doctor. How long would the wait be? Would we be surrounded by a lot of other ill individuals in the waiting room? I knew there were a lot of different viruses going around, and I didn't want Joy to pick up anything else while she was at the doctor's office, or for us to bring home any viruses that would make the entire family sick. Besides, I needed to stay healthy for the upcoming meet.

> **You will show me the path of life; in Your presence is fullness of joy; at Your right hand are pleasures forevermore.**
>
> **—PSALM 16:11 (NKJV)**

I quickly scheduled a doctor's appointment and notified Joy's preschool she'd be absent for the day. As we went to get into the van, I got an email from the preschool director to all the families in Joy's class explaining that there was strep throat exposure. While Joy didn't have any strep symptoms, I thought, *God, please help me to remember to ask the doctor to do a strep test.* I was beginning to see God's hand over the whole day.

We made our way into the clinic. There were only a couple of people in the waiting room, allaying my fears about exposure to other viruses. We barely waited five minutes before Joy's name was called.

The doctor looked at Joy's ears and confirmed she had an ear infection. As the doctor set up a prescription for an antibiotic, I remembered my other worry. "Before leaving the house, I saw an email from Joy's preschool that she was exposed to strep throat in her class. Can we please test her for it?"

The nurse gave Joy a strep test and then we were on our way home. The entire appointment, including travel, had only taken 45 minutes! What an amazing answer to prayers!

My husband, Kyle, decided to work from home that day and I realized that I could get my workout done at the YMCA after all. So I left Joy with him and went to the pharmacy to have the prescription filled, then came back home to give Joy the first dose. Afterward, I finally made it to the YMCA for a later-than-usual workout. Within 10 minutes of being at the Y, I received a phone call that Joy had tested positive for strep.

I prayed, *Lord, thank You for the timing of the preschool director's email. Thank You for giving us the insight we needed to help Joy get the best care while at the clinic.*

> **May the God of hope fill you with all joy and peace as you trust in him, so that you may overflow with hope by the power of the Holy Spirit.**
>
> —ROMANS 15:13 (NIV)

I was able to get through my whole workout, then went downstairs through the pool area and into the sauna. As I was sitting and sweating, I looked out the glass windows. *Is that who I think it is?*

Weeks prior, I had seen my friend Vanessa at the pool I train at for masters swimming. She had a lot going on in her life, including the loss of a close family member and the ending of a close friendship. As a single mom, she cared for two children still living at home. I knew it was all weighing heavily on her. It was just a few days ago that I had been thinking about her, but I hadn't had a chance to call and catch up.

> **Trust in the LORD with all your heart and lean not on your own understanding; in all your ways submit to him, and he will make your paths straight.**
>
> —PROVERBS 3:5–6 (NIV)

I left the sauna and walked down the side of the pool to get Vanessa's attention. When she finally stopped at the side of the pool, I sat down on the floor nearby. "Vanessa, I have been thinking about you a lot. I've been praying for you. How are you?"

"It's good to see you," she said with tears in her eyes. "The past few nights I have barely slept. My kids are keeping me going. But last night I slept a few hours straight. I woke up feeling good, and I wanted to go for a swim. It feels great to be here."

Vanessa let me pray for her. As I did, I prayed that God would touch her with His presence. In that moment, the Holy Spirit helped me remember almost word-for-word Psalm 16:11, and I prayed that over her. I felt that our interaction was a God-incidence—a divine miracle orchestrated by God. As I left the Y, I sensed that everything that had happened earlier with my daughter and the morning delay was God at work, leading me to touch the life of a friend who desperately needed some encouragement and prayer.

The rest of the week my family and I went back to our normal weekly routine. Joy was starting to feel a lot better, and nobody else in the house got sick.

That Sunday, after church service, I went for a walk in our neighborhood. It was a beautiful November day. I walked down a street I hadn't been down in quite a while. I was reflecting and praying about the week, my interaction with Vanessa, Joy's health, writing projects I was working on, and the upcoming swim meet. I rounded the corner and happened to be looking down when I spotted a card with a dog and a cat pictured on the front. I was curious, so I picked it up and realized it was a completely unused birthday card. There was no handwritten message in it, but printed in the card was Psalm 16:11—the same verse I had prayed over Vanessa!

Shocked, I laughed out loud with joy. I felt delight in God's presence in a way that I hadn't experienced before. The seemingly random encounters with Psalm 16:11 gave me a peace and an assurance that I can trust God in the day-to-day, even when things happen that are completely out of my control. I felt lifted by His Word, marveling at the blessings in the series of events that were divinely orchestrated just days prior.

Serving the Lord in Every Season

Laura Bailey

I slapped the alarm clock, questioning why I continued to set it each night, knowing I would already be awake. I wriggled free of my finally snoozing baby, stealthily placing her in her crib, and shuffled my way to the kitchen. As I waited for that first hit of caffeine to jolt me awake, I opened my Bible and prayed my daughter would sleep a little longer.

It had been almost a year of sleepless nights and restless days. The Sandman only seemed to visit my little one when I was holding her, and only for 2-hour increments, while the sun was shining. I was exhausted physically, mentally, emotionally, and spiritually. I struggled to maintain a consistent quiet time, and even when I did read my Bible, shamefully, I would often doze off.

For Christmas, a friend gave me a yearly devotional. Each day held a verse, a word of encouragement, and a prayer. I removed my bookmark from its place (two months behind today's date) and began reading. Romans 12:1 was the verse: "Therefore, I urge you, brothers and sisters, in view of God's mercy, to offer your bodies as a living sacrifice, holy and pleasing to God—this is your true and proper worship" (NIV). The author shared that each day is an opportunity to sacrifice ourselves to serve the Lord and His Kingdom. Our Heavenly

Father places numerous opportunities in our paths to serve and honor Him in every season and circumstance.

I wiped away a tear that escaped down my cheek. I'd left my job recently to stay home with my girls and was floundering in this new role. I felt the Lord stirring my heart to do something more. But I could barely stay awake long enough to read a 5-minute devotional. What could I offer the Lord in this season that was occupied with children, where I had little margin in my day?

> **Do not conform to the pattern of this world, but be transformed by the renewing of your mind. Then you will be able to test and approve what God's will is—his good, pleasing and perfect will.**
>
> **—ROMANS 12:2 (NIV)**

Most days, I worked on autopilot. I didn't even remember the date until a friend texted me that evening. "Don't forget, new Bible study starts tonight."

Tonight's Wednesday? I didn't think I had the energy to go. I would just pretend I hadn't seen the message. But when the time rolled around to leave for Bible study, I decided to go after all. The day had been tough. I could get some relief, if only for an hour, by placing my wailing daughter in the nursery, and then my husband and I would be headed to church.

I was surprised to see our pastor greeting us as we entered the room. *He doesn't usually teach small-group Bible study. And why is there a blank sheet of paper at each seat? I hope this isn't going to involve a lot of mental energy. I was looking forward to just taking it easy tonight.*

The pastor shared that the usual teacher was sick, and he was filling in tonight. Then he gave us our assignment for the evening: "Open your Bibles to Romans 12:1 and take a few minutes to meditate on this verse. Then, rewrite it in your own words."

My head snapped up. Usually, I would be anxious about this sort of activity. I'd grown up in church but was quite inexperienced in Bible knowledge and interpretation. But, staring at the blank page, I felt the gentle heart nudge of the Holy Spirit inviting me to press into the exercise. It wasn't a coincidence that this was the same verse from my devotions this morning.

I flipped open my Bible, the ribbons still holding the spot from earlier, and reread Romans 12:1.

> **Through Jesus, therefore, let us continually offer to God a sacrifice of praise—the fruit of lips that openly profess his name. And do not forget to do good and to share with others, for with such sacrifices God is pleased.**
>
> —HEBREWS 13:15–16 (NIV)

Glancing over previous chapters, I made a connection: "therefore," the first word of the verse, referred back to Romans 11:36, which states that *all* things are from God, through God, and for God. "Therefore," believers should live their lives in light of this.

Now, what, exactly, is God's "mercy"? God is sending His only Son to take *my* undeniably deserved place on the cross.

Jesus paid the price for *my* sin; He took *my* punishment and by His *amazing* grace, He saved me from condemnation and offered me eternal life in His glorious kingdom. *Therefore*, I am to offer myself as a sacrifice to Him, to be used as an instrument of worship and service. *Therefore*, according to the riches I enjoy because of God's mercy, He requires me to be pure and holy as I serve Him through worship, thanksgiving, and obedience.

> **May these words of my mouth and this meditation of my heart be pleasing in your sight, Lord, my Rock and my Redeemer.**
>
> **—PSALM 19:14 (NIV)**

As I finished writing, the reality of God's mercy suddenly overcame me. Words I had breezed through multiple times while reading this passage suddenly transitioned from mere script typed on a page to God's living Word tattooed on my heart.

Once everyone had an opportunity to write down their thoughts, our pastor asked if anyone would share what they wrote. Not normally one to shy away from sharing, and usually the first to raise a hand, I stared at my page, my hands glued to my sides.

"Laura, you seemed to be feverishly writing. Would you mind sharing what the Lord laid on your heart?"

Seriously? Out of all the people in the room, why do I have to be the one to share? Taking a deep breath, I began to read.

"Laura, lean in, listen closely; this is important, and I want to ensure that you clearly understand what I am about to say. You are loved by God so much that instead of giving you what you deserve, death, God will give you eternal life through the

GOD'S GIFT OF TOUCH
— Eryn Lynum —

A GEODE DOESN'T look like much from the outside. If you run your fingers over it, you get the sensation of a rough, dull rock, but inside, they are filled with breathtaking crystals. What starts as an unremarkable void is transformed as water seeps through the rock's porous outer shell, allowing minerals to accumulate inside and gradually grow into crystals.

Jesus provides eternally satisfying water. John 7:38 (NIV) says, "Whoever believes in me, as Scripture has said, rivers of living water will flow from within them." At the touch of His living water, emptiness is replaced by stunning, multifaceted beauty.

---

sacrifice of His son, Jesus. Acknowledging this reality that God spared you from the eternal consequences of sin, through your acceptance of Jesus Christ as Lord and Savior, you are to offer every part of your life to the Lord.

"Laura, you can please God by surrendering yourself each day to be used for His Glory. Every day is different, and the opportunities to bring God glory are endless. Each act of service is significant in God's Kingdom. The Lord takes delight when you care for family or take a meal to a neighbor and when you get up early and spend time with Him, even when your eyelids begin to droop. You are serving and honoring the Lord in this season. True worship stems from our heart's motivations, not just outward actions."

Tears escaped my eyes again; the drops sprinkled my page. Twice in one day, I was moved by the presence of the Holy

Spirit. It was no coincidence that the Lord placed Romans 12:1 in my path twice, a reminder by a loving Father to accept the grace and mercy He so lavishly bestows on His children. God didn't need more of my doing for Him; He desires my heart.

Many years have passed since that day, and now, thankfully, my little girl sleeps through the night! But, even in this new season, life offers new distractions and busyness. When I start to feel that I am not "doing enough" or I've "failed God," I get out my piece of paper and remind myself of the remarkable truth of the Gospel "in view of God's mercy."

God Showed Himself to Me through My Friend

Sandra Fischer

Can a believer of Christ go through a lifetime without experiencing how God shows His presence in personal, definable ways? I don't believe so. For me, the way God assured me of His presence and care was through a person—my dear friend, Marlene.

Marlene was one of the first people to welcome me into the small town where I settled upon marrying my husband. We attended the same church, had the same circle of friends, and socialized together often. She was a wonderful woman of faith, and full of spiritual wisdom. At first, that was sometimes annoying to me. While I professed to be a Christian and demonstrated the appearance of knowing Christ, she saw through my hypocrisy. She was patient, kind, loving, and faithful, and she prayed for me. After 15 years, God answered her prayer. My life was in crisis, and when I cried out to God in desperation to help me, He sent Marlene. She had begged me to go to a women's retreat many times, but this time was God's time, and I assented to go.

The theme of the retreat was "Lord, Change Me." What a revelation to learn that I was the problem, and I needed a life change. I prayed for Christ to make me His. Through the power of the Holy Spirit in me, I was able to read the Bible with His guidance and understanding. My life began to change. Marlene and I started meeting regularly to share our spiritual journey. She became my prayer partner, my accountability sister. We met weekly, and our conversations turned from talking about our children's activities or vacation plans to what was happening in us spiritually.

Years passed, and as we grew older, we began to think about the aging process and the end of life. We talked about which nursing home our children might place us in and which one we'd prefer. We'd insist on being together, a group home, and we would be residents of grace. We would keep wearing makeup even if our mascara smeared or our lipstick was crooked. Our clothes would be colorful, flashy, and silky to complement our gray hair. Our talk would be about pleasant memories punctuated with giggles—no groaning or complaining even if our bodies objected. Marlene had a wonderful sense of humor, and we laughed as we made our plans. Little did we know then that God had a different plan and a different group home in mind for Marlene.

Not long after we celebrated Marlene's sixty-second birthday, one of our friends rushed into my office to say Marlene had been taken to the hospital, confused and glassy-eyed. The description sounded like a stroke, but we learned she was to have emergency brain surgery for a tumor in her front lobe the size of an orange.

Another close friend and I went to visit her the next day. She was propped up in bed with gauze wrapped around her head like a turban. Her demeanor was typical of her affable personality. "Well, I guess I gave them a piece of my mind," she said with a smile. Her comment was a momentary diffusion of our uneasiness.

Weeks followed with many MRIs, various other scans, and radiation treatments. The prognosis indicated the tumor would return despite the efforts to stem it. Her head was shaved in the front so they could mark it for the treatments, so we helped shop for wigs and hats. She wore them at first, but then discarded them as nuisances. She said she wanted people to forsake the idea that her body was the most important part of her.

Marlene's eyes of faith rested on something far beyond the parameters of this world. Her perceptive vision of what lay ahead would be confirmed by the God of Glory Himself. One October day, several months later, during church, I looked across the sanctuary at her. Her shiny forehead with the purple markings was bowed; I looked away, my heart stricken. I turned the pages of the hymnal I held to scriptures in the back, and this one caught my eye: "Whom have I in heaven but you? And there is nothing on earth that I desire besides you. My flesh and my heart may fail, but God is the strength of my heart and my portion forever" (Psalm 73:25–26, ESV). I opened my Bible to the reference and wrote Marlene's name and the date beside it.

> **Whom have I in heaven but you? And there is nothing on earth that I desire besides you. My flesh and my heart may fail, but God is the strength of my heart and my portion forever.**
>
> —PSALM 73:25–26 (ESV)

The new year came, and with it were prayer meetings and laying on of hands for Marlene, but she was at peace. She did require constant companionship and supervision as time went on because she had dizzy spells and lapses of memory. Her husband insisted on keeping her home and caring for her, so many of us volunteered to help by taking turns to stay with her while he went to work. One of my days happened to be on her birthday, so I asked her what special thing we could do that day to celebrate. In her inimitable way, she cocked her head and smiled. "Want to go get an MRI?" We both doubled over.

> **So we do not lose heart. Though our outer self is wasting away, our inner self is being renewed day by day. For this light momentary affliction is preparing for us an eternal weight of glory beyond all comparison.**
>
> —2 CORINTHIANS 4:16–17 (ESV)

In April, my husband and I retired and moved south to a new home miles away. Marlene and Duane were the last two people we visited before we left. She was hunched over in a wheelchair and couldn't speak, but she managed a goodbye smile. Within a few short weeks, we heard she was failing.

On May 24, Duane called us to say her passing was near. He asked if I had a copy of the *Our Daily Bread* devotional, one that Marlene and I had read and shared together for years. He said she had been reading days ahead in her copy and had highlighted several pages and verses. "Look at the one for May 26."

I opened the devotional and read. I gasped. The scripture was Psalm 73:25–26! Then I told Duane about what I had written in my Bible 7 months before. We both wept.

I knew that God had been present when the psalmist wrote that verse, when my Bible and the hymnal were published, and when the devotional was prepared. He was present with Marlene when she was reading the days ahead and highlighted that verse from Psalms. And He was present with Marlene on May 26, the date of the devotion with that particular scripture— and the day that she passed into His heavenly presence.

We returned for Marlene's memorial celebration, and Duane shared more evidence of how God manifests Himself. When he called the pastor to plan the memorial, the pastor said, "I prayed for what scriptures I might use. There are many common ones, but I was drawn to one that is a little different, that speaks to Marlene."

I didn't have to ask; I knew. And Duane confirmed, yes, it was Psalm 73:25–26.

God knew Marlene and she knew Him. His marvelous grace in showing Himself in her life and through her death is a treasure upon which my confidence rests. He says He will show Himself to all who seek Him. He did, He does, and He will.

When Google Brought Me God's Message

Chelsea Ohlemiller

It was my birthday, a day that should be joyful and celebratory. Instead, it was full of grief. The woman who made it all possible, the woman who did all of the hard and important work, was no longer here to make it feel special. My mother died several years ago, and while this wasn't my first birthday without her, it still held the same profound emptiness.

In ache and longing, desperate for wisdom and comfort, I searched intentionally in the place you search for anything these days: Google.

I don't remember what I searched for, or the exact phrase I typed onto my computer screen, except that it was nothing to do with faith. There were no words like God, scripture, Bible, or verse. I don't remember what I was hoping to find, only that my heart was searching for comfort, desperate for something that could guide me like my mother once had, with love and compassion and exuberant encouragement.

After hitting enter on my keyboard, the side of my computer screen lit up with the words of Proverbs 3:5 (KJV): "Trust in the LORD with all thine heart; and lean not unto thine own understanding."

It wasn't only the words that caught my eye. The number had a special significance for me because my birthday is March 5: 3-5. How had a verse so numerically tied to me, so spiritually significant, appeared on my screen when they had nothing to do with the words I'd used to initiate the search? There are certain things in life that allow God to remain anonymous, showing up like a coincidence, communicating in unexpected, yet undeniable, ways. This was one of them.

I read the words over and over again, tears streaming from my face. Since my mother passed, things like this seemed to happen often. When I feel distanced from her and in need of her motherly guidance, pieces of her would arrive, reminding me of her love and her influence. In times when my faith felt unsteady or even in direct conflict with my mind and comprehension, God always showed up in a way that simply cannot be ignored, that says, *God is with you always.*

On that day, God showed up for me boldly in the numerals that matched the day I was born, 3:5. It turns out that you don't have to search for scripture to uplift your soul when it's been delicately woven into your existence, for it sits there with you always.

These invaluable words of counsel and enlightenment appeared without opening my Bible. They appeared without me entering any type of phrase that would create a response like the one in front of me, yet there they were. And in all truth, even better, there He was—God.

I had an undeniable reminder in front of me that He is always present, always championing me from afar. He's always lifting us up, even when we feel like we're in pain as deep as the ocean or grief as heavy as dirt from 6 feet under. He's always showing up for us, even when we give the credit to someone or something easier to accept, and even when we fail to acknowledge His display of love and direction.

This simple search, with profound answers, made it abundantly clear who I should be seeking—not Google, but God. I had my efforts placed in the wrong influence, the wrong guidance, and tried to use human means to comprehend things I wasn't fully able to understand, for grief cannot be conquered or won.

Until that moment, on my birthday, I had never heard those words or that particular scripture. I never knew the way my faith and God's Word had been linked. Now, those words are etched into my notebook. They're highlighted in my Bible, with doodles and inspiration. They're in my heart, as a constant reminder of the unexpected way God's hand is in all that I am and all that I do.

Even with this powerful display of God's presence and insight, will I always wonder why things had to be this way? Will I always search for my mother's comfort and guidance? Will I always ask questions of God and my faith? I'm not sure, but being the imperfect human that I am, I probably will. And that's OK. Each time, I will be reminded of His presence, His comfort, and His promises. His Word tells me I'm never alone. *We* are never alone. God is here in ways we cannot see and by means we simply cannot comprehend. He will be creative in His approach when He needs to be, always remaining anonymous and invisible, yet always bold in intent. All we have to do is be open to His messages and His love. If we are, we'll see they're sent just for us when we need them the most. No mistake, no coincidence—only God.

O Holy Spirit, descend
plentifully into my heart.
Enlighten the dark corners
of this neglected dwelling
and scatter there Thy
cheerful beams.

—Saint Augustine

CHAPTER 2

Calling Out to God

Our Eyes Are on You

Mindy Baker

As my parents have grown older, the changes in their health have become increasingly debilitating. A few years ago, my dad was diagnosed with progressive supranuclear palsy (PSP), which is a brain disease that affects the ability to balance, walk, and swallow. What started as subtle changes in both his personality and physical abilities slowly, over time, became more problematic. My mom had been doing her best to care for him in their home, but looking back, I don't think that my brother or I realized the degree of care that my dad had come to need. Due to Mom's own set of physical limitations, and the increasing progression of Dad's disease, catastrophe was inevitable. And when it struck, it left us all in shock.

In the months leading up to this situation, Dad had fallen several times, and each time Mom had somehow been able to help him back into a chair or bed. One time a neighbor was there to assist. However, on this occasion, he tripped and fell on top of her, fracturing some of her ribs. After a trip to the ER, she returned home, but in quite a bit of discomfort and unable to continue caring for my dad. I traveled to their home 8 hours away to help.

The night I arrived, my eyes were opened to the severity of the problem. Dad's needs were more drastic than Mom had been letting on, far beyond what she should have been attempting to manage on her own. That night, Mom woke up and wanted more pain medication to alleviate the pain in her ribs. She stumbled in the bathroom and fell. My dad, although bedridden, woke up and called out for help. I ran into their room and found her unconscious in a pool of blood, her injury made worse from the medication she was taking to prevent blood clotting.

I called 911 and the medics arrived. Fear gripped me as they loaded her up in an ambulance. I told my dad to stay put in the bed and that I would be back as quickly as I could. I had no choice but to leave him there and hope he would not put himself at risk by trying to move around on his own. As I followed the ambulance to the hospital in my car, panic began to rise in my heart. I did the only thing I could think to do: I prayed.

A verse that I had memorized months previously popped into my mind to help guide me in my prayers for help. The verse was 2 Chronicles 20:12 (NIV): "We do not know what to do, but our eyes are on you." When I cried out to God with this prayer, His supernatural peace flooded my heart. In that moment, I acknowledged my weakness and turned my worry over to Him.

> "We have no power to face this vast army that is attacking us. We do not know what to do, but our eyes are on you."
>
> —2 CHRONICLES 20:12 (NIV)

Once they stabilized Mom at the hospital, I drove back to my parents' home to care for Dad. At breakfast the next morning, I explained to him that Mom wouldn't be coming home for at least a few days. As I consulted with the doctors later that morning, I discovered that the healing process would actually require weeks in a rehabilitation facility. I had some important decisions to make about where my dad should live in both the short-term and the long-term, and I needed to figure it all out quickly. Besides being in an unfamiliar city, I had many questions and very few answers. I knew next to nothing about rehabilitation facilities, long-term nursing care, financial details, insurance coverage, or any of the other details I would have to work out to take care of both of my parents. I felt extremely overwhelmed and alone. I kept praying my verse, asking God to direct my steps. *I do not know what to do, but my eyes are on you, Lord.*

Over the course of the next week, I marveled at how God provided the right people and resources to assist me. I don't remember the name of the social worker who called me, but I believe she was sent by God to keep me calm and clear-minded. She was very knowledgeable. Together, we discussed and researched different options and made multiple calls to doctors, insurance representatives, and nursing facilities. And between all of the calls, I prayed.

In the end, I was able to find a double room in a nearby rehabilitation facility where both my mom and my dad could stay together. This facility had received many high reviews and was my number-one choice. The social worker told me how rare this was. In her experience, there were usually long waiting lists and red tape. We were able to arrange things so that once my mom was strong enough to return home, my dad could transfer to the other side of the facility, where they handled long-term care. In the meantime, we could start to put all of the financial arrangements into place. I felt relieved at this solution and very thankful to God for His provision.

But I hadn't told Dad the plan yet. Up until this point, with the exception of one previous short-term stay at a rehabilitation facility—one that had not gone well—he had always lived at home with my mom. I knew he wanted to continue living at home.

I dreaded telling him the news. *What do I say?* I wanted to promise him that this was only a short-term stay, but in my heart I knew that he would most likely *not* be returning home. His needs were too great for Mom to continue caring for him in the way she had been, and he would only need more care as his disease progressed. We had reached the point where it was necessary for him to live in a nursing home full-time. I felt extreme guilt as I packed up some of his clothes and belongings, and continued to make arrangements while he watched TV. *I don't know what to do, Lord, but my eyes are on You.*

> **Teach me to do your will, for you are my God; may your good Spirit lead me on level ground.**
>
> **—PSALM 143:10 (NIV)**

The next morning, I broke the news to him as gently as I could. I could see the shock and disappointment on his face, although he accepted it without too much fuss. The fact that he could stay with Mom until she healed seemed to soften the news slightly. "So this is it?" he asked. "Is there a chance I could come home?"

I didn't want to make false promises, so I said quietly, "I don't know, Dad." We talked briefly about the physical therapy he would receive at the facility, which might help, but we both knew the downward spiral of PSP that he was experiencing. Returning home wasn't a reality.

Soon after, we loaded up in the car and drove to the nursing home and got him settled. The whole experience seemed surreal.

In the moment I stayed strong, but later, after dropping him off, I wept. I longed for a different outcome. *Why, Lord?* There was no answer. Nor would there be until heaven. But in the midst of all the chaos and confusion that swirled in my mind, I held on to my verse. I knew without a doubt that God had helped me to put a plan into place so that my parents would be safe and well cared for before I returned home. I marveled at how He led me one step at a time. I thanked God for His direction, presence, and provision.

The Everyday Miracle of a Sunrise

Lynne Hartke

Seven glorious days at our cabin in northern Arizona stretched before me. I could hardly wait! I had rearranged my schedule so I could do my writing and other work while enjoying the cooler weather in the old-growth forest of blue spruce, ponderosa pines, and cedar.

A personal goal was also on the agenda: to photograph the sunrise in twenty-five locations over the summer months. The cabin would be a perfect place to kick-start the project.

My photography list included a drive to Mormon Lake to capture the ravens soaring on the wind currents, calling out their scratchy croaks. I hoped to get a picture of the stellar jays from the back deck as they scolded me from the branches of the pines until I tossed out a handful of peanuts. I wanted to photograph the elk herd who came for a morning drink at the fresh spring on the western edge of the lake. In the past, I had watched as mamas called to their young while the calves frolicked in the shallow water. The scenic overlook also made the list, where the wildflowers bent in the morning breeze—red penstemon, orange globemallow, and yellow sunflowers. The backdrop for all the photos would be the rising sun.

The idea of photographing twenty-five different sunrises developed while I recovered from a nasty virus that had left me exhausted, with a bone-aching tiredness that had dogged me for months. In order to function, I required 9 hours of sleep each night and a nap during the day. Once an avid hiker, my daily exercise had been reduced to a stroll around the neighborhood. Sometimes even that was too much.

With my limited energy, I had fallen into a poor-me funk, until I came up with the plan to photograph the twenty-five sunrises. I might not be able to hike to beautiful places, but I could drive to them. Now at the cabin, I planned to take the first photo the following morning. Maybe of the elk herd!

> **Light is sown for the righteous, and joy for the upright in heart. Rejoice in the LORD, O you righteous, and give thanks to his holy name!**
>
> —PSALM 97:11–12 (ESV)

Tired from the drive and needing to catch my breath in the higher altitude, I headed to the back deck.

No sooner had I settled into a chair with a hot cup of Earl Grey than my husband, Kevin, texted: *They are closing the forest.*

I stared at my phone in disbelief. *What? Who is closing the forest?* I texted back.

I'll send you the link.

My heart sank as I read the announcement from Coconino National Forest officials, our landlords, so to speak. Our cabin is located on US Forest Service land in a unique partnership. If they closed the forest, we could not access the cabin.

Coconino National Forest covers 1.856 million acres. Not only our cabin, but some of the state's most popular recreation areas lie within the borders, including the red rocks of Sedona and the aspen-lined trails of the San Francisco peaks near Flagstaff. The forest is a great place to escape the triple-digit heat of Phoenix, but the unending high temperatures, combined with low rainfall, had created tinder box conditions. Fourteen large wildfires burned in the state, including the nearby Rafael Fire that cloaked Flagstaff—the closest large city—in smoke. Caused by a lightning strike, the fire had burned more than 36,000 acres and remained uncontained, despite firefighting efforts.

> **Send out your light and your truth; let them lead me; let them bring me to your holy hill and to your dwelling!**
>
> **—PSALM 43:3 (ESV)**

With firefighters and personnel stretched too thin, the US Forest Service made the difficult decision to fully close the forest. "There's just too much at risk," an official declared. "We have limited resources, and we're tapped out."

What are you going to do? Kevin texted.

I guess I am coming home. My weeklong stay was over before it had begun. I repacked the car for a turnaround trip while our dog, Mollie, pranced around me. A few hours later, I gave a wave to our nearby neighbor, Ted.

"Are you ready to take off?" Ted called from his driveway. He shoved another suitcase into his stuffed truck. He walked over for a closer chat. "The forest closes tomorrow," he reminded me, wiping sweat from his forehead.

"I'm leaving in the morning," I said, "after a good night's sleep."

"These cabins have lasted almost one hundred Arizona summers. They've survived other wildfire seasons," he reasoned, trying to lift the mood. "We will be back again when the forest reopens."

I turned to look at our small cabin, which had been built in the 1920s. I loved its one cozy bedroom and the massive stone fireplace in the living room. We had owned it for only 2 years—a welcome summer retreat from our busy schedules. I agreed with Ted, hoping his prediction was true. With a final wave, he strode back to his truck. I watched his taillights as he drove away.

Ted was the last neighbor to leave. Mollie and I were alone on the mountain. I loaded a few more items into the truck and headed to bed. The packing and emotional upheaval had sapped my energy. I sank into my pillow with a relieved sigh.

But sleep eluded me. The smoke from the fires drifted into my dreams, impairing my breathing. In the suffocating air, every sound was magnified. After hours of tossing, I threw aside the blankets and stepped outside in the predawn morning.

The skies over the distant lakebed belonged to another world. Hazy. Gray. Heavy. Like a dingy wool blanket that had seen too much wear-and-tear and needed to be thrown out.

No birds sang from the trees. No chipmunks scurried on the forest floor searching for acorns among the pine needles. No elk bugled or called to their young.

Absolute silence greeted me. Like a heavy shroud.

The wind had shifted during the night. Ash fell like rain on the deck where I stood. It was time to go. I did not need to call Mollie twice.

Within minutes we joined a long line of campers and trucks heading south toward Phoenix. Boats and other recreational equipment filled the accompanying trailers. The sun was just beginning to rise—a murky-red orb suspended over the smoke-filled horizon, like an apocalyptic messenger. I wondered when—or if—we would return.

Once home, life returned to normal work schedules, my plan to photograph the sunrises shelved with the extra boxes of stuff I had packed from the cabin. After all, who wanted photos of ordinary routines and everyday life? My poor-me funk returned as well.

Scrolling through my phone one afternoon, a meme with a Bible verse caught my attention: "But this I call to mind, and therefore I have hope: The steadfast love of the LORD never ceases; his mercies never come to an end; they are new every morning; great is your faithfulness" (Lamentations 3:21–23, ESV).

> **The steadfast love of the LORD never ceases; his mercies never come to an end; they are new every morning; great is your faithfulness.**
>
> —LAMENTATIONS 3:21–23 (ESV)

Call to mind. I wouldn't need to call to mind if it was easy to remember. I decided it was time to remind myself of God's faithfulness. Of His unending mercy that was new every morning. It was time to photograph the sunrise.

In the days that followed, I photographed the sun from a swing set at a city park. I caught the sun's reflection in a puddle made by sprinklers on the sidewalk. City landmarks and

GOD'S GIFT OF TOUCH
— Lynne Hartke —

BUTTERFLIES NEED THE warming touch of the sun. Their cold-blooded bodies require temperatures of at least 60 degrees (but prefer 82 to 100 degrees) before taking flight. Without the touch of the sun, butterflies will tuck themselves under structures or plants until the temperature rises. Butterflies also bask in sunny spots, their wings spread wide to soak up the sun's rays. Psalm 19:6 (NIV) says of the sun, "It rises at one end of the heavens and makes its circuit to the other; nothing is deprived of its warmth." Like butterflies, humans can also spread their arms wide in gratitude with the warmth of the sun—and the Son.

---

towering cactus made other shots. When I didn't go for a drive, I opened the blinds on the front window and welcomed the sun coming up in the neighborhood.

Ordinary, repetitive days.

I called to mind God's faithfulness as I continued to gain strength from my illness. I called to mind His mercy as the Rafael fire continued to rage. Over 75,000 acres. New fires sprang up. For 16 days, Kevin and I watched the weather and fire updates for Coconino National Forest. For 16 days, we *called to mind*.

Each day I reflected on God's love as I got up to greet the sun. The daily waking to the 24-hour rhythm spoke to the depths of my soul. Obviously, the sun had been coming up since the beginning of creation, yet for the first time in my life, I made a point of being a witness to its rising. I found hope returning to all my hidden places where doubts had taken root.

"Did you hear?" Kevin asked on day seventeen, when I was searching for my keys for a drive to greet the sun. "Drenching rains have come. We can return to the cabin this weekend."

"The fires?"

"Contained or manageable."

I bowed my head in thanks before turning to open the blinds on the front window. A northern mockingbird sang from our neighbor's palm tree. An emerald-throated hummingbird flitted by our feeder. I snapped a photo as the first beams of light radiated across a tangerine sky. I stood as a witness to the end of darkness and the arrival of light.

An everyday miracle.

We're Not Going If You're Not!

Tina Wanamaker

I had been preparing for 2 months to teach at a retreat week-end for women, and finally it was here. The opening session the night before had gone well, as had the second session, which had just concluded. Much prayer and study undergirded the weekend, and the attendees were lovely and desiring to hear from the Lord.

After that morning session, I spent time ministering and then retired to my room before lunch. I would have another session after lunch and one in the evening, and the closing session the next morning, which made a total of five sessions to share what God had laid on my heart for these ladies. A sudden wave of doubt came over me. *I can't do this.* Not in my own strength. Not with my own words.

In my recent quiet time with the Lord, I had been studying Exodus 33, where Moses spoke with God face-to-face. The Israelites had just left Egypt and were facing a long, hard trek to their new home, the "land of milk and honey," as it says in 33:3 (NIV). At the beginning of the chapter, the Lord tells Moses that He will not go with the Israelites; they must make the trip alone. But Moses protests. It's no good for them to go if God isn't with them, he says. If God wasn't going, then he and the Israelites weren't going either.

This struck a chord within me, and I had been contemplating that on a personal level, considering my need of God's presence. The Lord had told Moses that He would take care of him and the people. He would send an angel before them. He would remove their enemies. He would make a way for them. But it was the presence of God that Moses desired more.

I knew I could show up at the coming sessions, teach the Word of God, answer questions, be present, pray with them, and point them to Jesus—but if it was just me, it wouldn't work. The women didn't need to see Tina. They didn't need my words or presence. They needed to see the Lord, to hear His words, and to be in His presence.

It wasn't that the retreat had been lacking in God's presence so far, but how could we bring an even greater sense of His presence into our activities? I needed

> **Then Moses said to him, "If your Presence does not go with us, do not send us up from here."**
>
> —EXODUS 33:15 (NIV)

Him. We needed Him. It's in His presence that we find fullness of joy and healing. It's in His presence that we find out who He is and who we are.

These thoughts brought me to the cabin floor. I bowed low before God and cried out to Him, "Lord, I need You! If You don't go, I don't want to go! It's pointless for me to go if Your presence doesn't go with me. I'm not going if You're not." I only had about 15 minutes before lunch was served, but in that time I poured my heart out to the Lord. I stayed on my knees, pleading with Him to be present and to do the ministry that was His to do. "Lord, please allow Your presence to go with me," I prayed.

Then I slowly rose and made myself presentable, gathered my Bible and notes, and stepped out of the room. When I arrived at the dining hall, women were finding their tables.

> **Now to him who is able to do immeasurably more than all we ask or imagine, according to his power that is at work within us, to him be glory.**
>
> —EPHESIANS 3:20–21 (NIV)

Name cards had been placed at the seats, and as I walked around looking for mine, I greeted the others. I finally saw the card with my name and sat down.

Once seated, I noticed another card bearing a scripture verse on my plate. I later learned that everyone had received a card with a verse that had been individually chosen and prayed over for each one in attendance. I picked up my card and read it.

"The LORD replied, 'My Presence will go with you, and I will give you rest'" (Exodus 33:14, NIV).

I sat there with that card in my hand, my awe growing as I realized the implications of it. The Lord was speaking to me directly. He was clearly telling me He was with me. And in addition to being with me, He was going to provide His rest as He accomplished His purpose in ministry to the women. Thankfully, no one else had sat down at my table yet, because tears pooled in my eyes. *How, Lord? How did You do this?*

For this to occur, the Lord had to have been at work weeks before, when the retreat organizers were praying over the verses. He would have been in their hearts, leading them to this specific verse and giving confirmation over it. In addition, He had been at work in my heart, too, bringing me to the spiritual state of mind that brought me to the cabin floor 15 minutes prior to sitting down at the table. He had known it all—the passage I'd been studying, the women who chose the verse, the spot at the table, each woman who would be present, the words to be spoken, and the confirmation I would need that He was with me and us as a group.

His presence was with me. He was with me. He would continue to minister in the way He desired to. He would accomplish His purpose. And in the midst of all of that, He would provide me with His rest.

The rest of my sessions were blessed by the Lord. He accomplished His purpose in the hearts of everyone there. There was laughter, tears, hugs, prayer, and ministry. Hearts were knit together. Difficult things were discussed. And in the midst of it all, God was with us. And it was His presence that made the difference. It's His presence that covers and gives life. God had orchestrated all of this—from the initial invitation to each detail to the very end.

That verse card was a direct answer from God. It lifted my head and reminded me that He was with me. It was just what I needed, straight from a very personal God. It wasn't just for me, though. It was for each woman who was present at the retreat. He provided not just His leading, but also His presence and His rest. He truly is able to do abundantly more than we ask or think.

The Shadow of Death

Heather Jepsen

After my hysterectomy, I thought the healing process was going fine—until suddenly it wasn't.

In the days immediately following the surgery, I was feeling great. I was happy to be recovering in comfort surrounded by my family and my pets. With cats and puppies on my lap, and even my mother to stop by and check on me, everything seemed good. But strangely, every now and then I would get really cold. I thought maybe it was because my uterus was gone. *Maybe I'm having a cold flash, the opposite of a hot flash,* I thought. It was probably nothing.

As time went by, I had more and more of these intense cold spells. I was shivering all the time, wrapping myself in blankets and putting "hot hands" packets in the bed with me. *Why can't I warm up?* I wondered. I checked my temperature, but there was no fever. I looked at my incision sites, and there was no redness or sign of infection. So I just decided it was some strange hormone thing and dismissed it.

At my 2-week post-op visit, I mentioned the cold spells to my doctor. She hadn't heard of those symptoms before but didn't seem worried. Then, on my way out the door, she stopped me. "Just pop over and get a blood test," she said. "It's probably nothing, but I want to be sure."

I had my blood drawn and left, not worried at all. I thought, *She's not worried, so I shouldn't be either.*

The next morning, after getting my kids off to school, I got a phone call. "Heather, your white blood cells are really high. I think you might have a hematoma in there from the surgery. Can you come do a CT scan today?"

"Sure," I said. I hadn't had breakfast yet, so I figured I'd just get it done.

I popped back over to the hospital, did the CT prep work, and had the scan. I still wasn't worried. I even saw one of my parishioners—when I'm not recovering from surgery, I'm a pastor—in the hospital waiting for a scan of her own. I stopped to chat with Clara about her situation. She told me they were worried about her heart. I told her about my scan, and we agreed to pray for each other.

I spent the day resting until it was time to pick up the kids from school. While I had my son in the car and we were waiting in line to get my daughter, I received a frantic call from my doctor.

> **The LORD is my shepherd; I shall not want. He makes me to lie down in green pastures; He leads me beside the still waters. He restores my soul.**
>
> **—PSALM 23:1–3 (NKJV)**

"Heather, your scan shows a huge infection in your abdomen. You need to get it drained as soon as possible. This is very serious. You can't get the work done at the hospital in town. You need to check in to the ER right now, have them transfer you by ambulance, and have a procedure to drain the infection at a hospital an hour away. You need to go to the ER immediately. I will tell them you are coming."

I was stunned. *An infection? ER right now? I don't have time for this! What am I going to do?* Tears welled up, but then I took a deep breath and got back to being a mom. We picked up my daughter and drove home. I called my husband to tell him he needed to drive me to the ER and drop me off.

The kids were scared out of their minds. "Are you going to die?" my son asked.

"No, I don't think so," I replied. "But I would have died if we didn't catch this. I just need to be in the hospital for a few days."

"What are we going to do?" my daughter asked. "Grandma is gone." *Oh no!* My mom was flying out of town that day to visit my brother.

As I waited for my husband to take me to the ER, I called my mom. "Mom, I have an infection," I said. "I need to go to the hospital."

"I'm coming back," my mom yelled into the phone. "I won't get on the plane."

"*No*, Mom," I said in the firmest voice I could muster, "you have to visit my brother. My family can do this. It will be OK. Just go." I ended up yelling at my mom to run back and catch her flight. It was awful, and I cried as I hung up the phone.

When my husband arrived at home, I hugged my kids to say goodbye. That was the hardest part. I knew I would see them again. But I also knew that this was serious. If I couldn't get the infection cleared, I was going to die.

My husband dropped me off at the ER and the big wait began. Then, I spotted Clara from church in the waiting room! Her doctors had been worried about her heart scan, so they sent her to the ER as well. She was seen before me, but when I finally got back to my room, she was right across the hall. Before I changed into my hospital gown, I went to her room and prayed with her. I prayed for myself too. God would be with us; we could do this.

The night was long, with lots of blood tests and waiting. Clara found out that she was going to be transferred to the same hospital as me. I smiled when I heard her say to the nurse, "Tell my pastor across the hall that I am going to the same hospital." The ambulance came and took Clara away, but still I waited.

As the night wore on, my spirit began to fail. The pain in my abdomen was getting worse and worse. I had been in the ER for 6 hours at this point, and I was thirsty, so I asked for water. When the nurse said no, I began to cry. It was just too much. Yelling at my mom, saying goodbye to my kids and husband,

He gives strength to the weary and increases the power of the weak.

—ISAIAH 40:29 (NIV)

being worried about myself, praying with Clara. I didn't want to be strong anymore. I just wanted to cry and let go.

A nurse came in and caught me crying. Instead of offering comfort, he gave me a lecture. "You are a pastor; you shouldn't be crying! This is a lesson God is teaching you. Buck up. Stop worrying. No crying." I wanted to tell him to leave me alone, but I just didn't have the spirit. I dried my eyes and hunkered down to wait for the ambulance. No sympathy in this ER.

At last, after 8 hours of waiting, it was time to transfer. I was loaded on the gurney and wheeled into the ambulance. The attendant left me alone as we rode an hour to the next hospital. In the dark and quiet night, I was finally free to let my tears fall. No one could see me here. I could release the stress and the fear and not be embarrassed or judged.

In my mind, I began to recite the twenty-third psalm (NKJV): *The LORD is my shepherd; I shall not want. . . . Yea, though I walk through the valley of the shadow of death, I will fear no evil; for You are with me . . .*

All of a sudden, I felt a presence at my side. I looked to see if it was the attendant, but the chair was empty. Still, I could feel someone there, next to me, holding my hand. I knew in my heart it was Jesus. He had come to offer me comfort when no one else could. He held my hand as I cried and cried. I had never felt so loved and comforted as I did in that ambulance. Jesus was there for me in a most profound way.

When we arrived at the second hospital, Jesus's presence was gone, but the comfort He offered me wasn't. I still had a long way to go, with painful procedures and a week's stay in the hospital ahead of me, but I never lost hope again. I knew God was with me. On the days when I was down, I would recite Psalm 23. Even though I was in the valley of death's shadow, I was not alone. In my darkest moment, in my lowest low, at my most alone and afraid, God was with me.

Flying the Friendly Skies

Adria Wilkins

I am not sure why I have always had a fear of flying. The process of flying fascinates me—the way that the power of the engine helps the plane move at high speeds, the way the air flow lifts the plane and keeps it in the air—but whenever I have to travel by plane, I tend to be anxious for days leading up to the flight and until I get to my destination.

In 1965, United Airlines had an advertising slogan that went, "Fly the friendly skies." United wanted people to think of flying as a safe and enjoyable experience. However, on my recent flight from Washington, DC, to Kentucky for a high-school reunion, the sky was anything but friendly.

For the first time in my life, I decided to get a first-class, front-row seat on my flight. I figured I deserved a little luxury. I boarded the plane and settled in, excited to be sitting up front and about the prospect of catching up with friends I had not seen for years. The flight attendant asked me if I would like a drink and a snack. I gladly accepted a Diet Coke and honey-roasted pistachios. It tasted like the best Diet Coke ever!

It was all going great as I enjoyed the view outside the window. But about 45 minutes into the flight, we began to experience turbulence. The unsteady movement of the plane did not subside. In fact, it got worse. The plane was shaking back and forth and making loud rattling noises. I knew it was serious when the flight attendants sat down and buckled up. They came on the intercom and said, "We will not be able to finish serving drinks and snacks. Please remain in your seats with your seat belt fastened. Put your trash in the pocket of the seat in front of you and we will gather it after you exit the plane."

> **Do not be anxious about anything, but in every situation, by prayer and petition, with thanksgiving, present your requests to God. And the peace of God, which transcends all understanding, will guard your hearts and your minds in Christ Jesus.**
>
> **—PHILIPPIANS 4:6–7 (NIV)**

I began to panic at the unsteady movement of the plane. Because I was in the front row, I had a wall in front of me, and the wall was moving violently back and forth. I closed my eyes. *Breathe,* I told myself. *You're in first class. Try to relax and enjoy it.*

It wasn't working. It had been a long time since I had a panic attack, but I felt one coming on. I knew I had to get my mind on something else.

A Bible passage I had memorized many years ago when I was dealing with high levels of anxiety in my life came to mind: Philippians 4:6–7 (NIV). I began mentally repeating the verses. *Do not be anxious about anything, but in every situation, by prayer and petition, with thanksgiving, present your requests to God. And the peace of God, which transcends all understanding, will guard your hearts and your minds in Christ Jesus.*

The verse has struck me in different ways throughout the years. At first, I'd had trouble remembering where the phrase "with thanksgiving" went; now, every time I get to that part, I stop and ponder being thankful. When praying for people, I would often quote verse 7: "And the peace of God, which transcends all understanding . . ."

But now, as panic threatened to swamp me again, it was the last part of that verse that stood out: ". . . will guard your hearts and your minds in Christ Jesus." The word *guard* made me stop and pause. I pictured someone guarding a door or a building. And why do they do that? To protect or control it.

I continued quoting those verses over and over during the bumpy ride. Every time I got

> **"Have I not commanded you? Be strong and courageous. Do not be afraid; do not be discouraged, for the LORD your God will be with you wherever you go."**
>
> —JOSHUA 1:9 (NIV)

to the word *guard*, I would stop. It felt as if God put a shield on my mind to protect me. My mind would stop thinking about the abrupt movements on the plane, and I would be at peace. I was not thinking about all the what–ifs, not allowing fears about the plane landing safely to take over my mind.

I could feel God's presence in my mind and surrounding me. It was as if His attention was totally focused on my mind and guarding me from heart palpations and shortness of breath.

And then we made it! The landing was hard and abrupt. I heard some people around me say, "If all flights were that way, no one would fly." I looked over at the man across the aisle, and he was taking some deep breaths.

As the airplane taxied up to the gate, I paused and thanked God for the safety He had provided for my mind as well as my body. God's presence filled the air that day. I felt Him guarding my mind and protecting me from anxiety.

When we invite God's presence into the storms in life, we do not have to be afraid. He promises to be with us, making the skies just a little bit friendlier.

No Time for Slumber

Linda Greene

I'm going insane.

I had attempted to sleep for hours, but the itching was so intense that it was once again keeping me awake. The rash that first appeared as a few tiny bumps on my belly now covered my torso and legs. The agonizing itch was worsening by the day, especially at night. Topical treatments didn't help, and oatmeal baths provided only temporary relief.

I was well into my second trimester, and in addition to the expected awkwardness of my big belly, I was contending with this relentless distress as well. Although it drove me crazy, my obstetrician was not concerned. He assured me this was not dangerous to my developing baby or me.

"This rash is most likely pregnancy-related, provoked by the hormones surging through your body." For safety reasons, he was not comfortable with prescribing any medication to alleviate these difficult-to-bear symptoms.

Great. As the doctor continued, I tried not to scratch my belly in front of him.

"At the very least, the rash should disappear in a few weeks once the baby is born."

What do I do until then? I pulled my shirt down as the appointment concluded.

As I scratched my legs, I thanked God that my checkups indicated I carried a healthy baby. Still, I felt horrible.

Since the time I learned I was expecting, I had suffered from one aggravating issue after another. First came the exhaustion and nausea. Later, test results showed I was borderline gestational diabetic. The doctor took that news in stride, monitoring me carefully, instructing me to watch my diet, and asking me to increase my exercise. Then, in the height of cold and flu season, I suffered from the worst sinus infection with a nagging cough that plagued me day and night. Now this.

> **I will not enter my house or go to my bed, I will allow no sleep to my eyes or slumber to my eyelids, till I find a place for the LORD.**
>
> —PSALM 132:3–5 (NIV)

I tossed and turned fitfully night after night. Amazingly, my husband slept through it all. I tried to avoid the temptation to glance at the clock, but that only made matters worse as my mind raced.

I gave in.

Oh, man. Only 3 more hours. Only 2. Ugh. How am I going to make it through the day? My firstborn, now a toddler, was due to get up soon.

Maybe I should get up and do a little reading. I need something to distract me from this torture. I tiptoed to my little corner office, where I wouldn't wake my son or hubby with the light. I surveyed the room, looking for something interesting to read. One book particularly caught my attention. My Bible. It had remained on my desk for a good portion of my pregnancy; I'd been too busy to give it too much attention.

Little one, I already love you so much, and it's a miracle how you're developing inside me, but you're depleting all my energy. I appreciated that fatigue was a good sign because that meant my body was working hard to grow a healthy baby. But I also spent my days chasing around our active little toddler, which added to my struggle to get through each day.

God understands, I thought to myself, justifying my lack of devotional time. *I haven't spent much time with Him lately, but He knows how I feel. I'm worn out and not doing well. I'll get back on track with my devotions once I feel better and sleep more. This spiritual inconsistency is just a short chapter in my life.*

It had been quite a while since I spent regular time with the Lord in the Word, and I realized that now that I was ready, I didn't know where to begin. *I'm usually involved in a Bible study, meditating on either a particular book of the Bible or a specific topical study. Lately, however, nothing!* I picked up my Bible and thumbed through it.

> **For the word of God is alive and active. Sharper than any double-edged sword, it penetrates even to dividing soul and spirit, joints and marrow; it judges the thoughts and attitudes of the heart.**
>
> —HEBREWS 4:12 (NIV)

Lord, what would You like me to read?

This night, I felt persuaded to read the Good Book from wherever I randomly opened it. Normally, my time in the Word was much more intentional and focused. Right then, however, that is what I felt the Lord wanted me to do.

"I will not enter my house or go to my bed, I will allow no sleep to my eyes or slumber to my eyelids, till I find a place for the LORD" (Psalm 132:3–5, NIV).

I sat there in silence, a sick feeling emanating from within. It was like God had highlighted that portion of Scripture just for me.

So, this is what they mean by God's Word being living and active. As a younger believer, I didn't even know that verse existed.

> **For the LORD disciplines those he loves, and he punishes each one he accepts as his child.**
>
> —HEBREWS 12:6 (NLT)

Right then and there, in the wee hours of the night, on the second floor of my home, I talked with God. He finally got my attention. I felt a lump in my throat as tears filled my eyes.

Oh, Lord, I am so sorry. You are a good, good Father. Now I understand the meaning behind You disciplining those You love. I feel so loved right now. I realize You have intentionally prevented me from sleeping because it's the only way to get me to listen. Lord, I know You understand that I'm tired and have a full schedule with my son, but I finally see how You miss spending time with me. I'm so sorry. I've been making excuses for my laziness, and in doing so, I've distanced myself from You. Without meaning to, I've been ignoring You. You just want some quality time with me. The God of all creation wished to spend time with *me.*

I knew God was disciplining me, but I never felt so cherished. I was convicted, not condemned. God's love was tangible and instructive that night. The One who held the universe in

GOD'S GIFT OF TASTE
— Terrie Todd —

THERE'S NOTHING LIKE a period of fasting to intensify the taste of food. Fresh tomatoes, watermelon, and buttered corn all come alive with flavor in ways not experienced when we're enjoying three square meals every day. No seasoning necessary!

Maybe the same is true in a spiritual sense. If we spend intentional, focused time with God—a "fast" from the business of everyday life—can we return to "regular life" with a heightened and profound appreciation for all His wonderful blessings? How could you taste the world in a different way?

His hand cared enough to take the time to redirect me and set me on a better path.

Please forgive me, Lord. From now on, I will intentionally set aside time for You. What a relational God!

My situation changed after that divine meeting with God. I went back to bed and drifted to sleep peacefully, without any itching. Over the next day or two, my rash vanished as quickly as it first appeared. God had taught me the lesson I needed to learn. As the Bible verse I opened to that night instructed me, I had found a place for my Lord.

Home Safe

Lois Hudson

Sometimes we don't recognize God's presence in our lives until we look back. I cared for my husband's mother in our home for 14 years, the last 7 of which she was bed-bound and non-verbal. Then, with no physical crisis as a warning, she passed away peacefully one night, at 95 years old.

We grieved, yet we had known that her condition was terminal; we were relieved that she was now in a better place. Slowly, we began to adjust to life after caregiving. It had been years since we'd had any sort of vacation, so I scheduled a getaway to our favorite retreat in the little Danish town of Solvang, California.

Before we traveled, my husband had his annual physical. We had thought it would be routine—just a formality—but instead we got some very bad news: two abdominal aneurysms. Consultations with specialists confirmed they were in danger of bursting. Surgery, though hazardous, was recommended.

The first specialist did nothing to alleviate our anxiety. He seemed to enjoy describing the procedure: surgical disconnection of every major organ from its arteries, repair of the aneurysms, and then reconnection of the arteries to their source.

"We could be in blood up to our ankles," was his terrifying pronouncement.

I immediately cancelled our reservations. We didn't want to be on the highway between towns searching for emergency care if the situation should "blow," as our less-than-subtle specialist put it.

Our primary-care physician apologized for the specialist's dramatics and sent us to another. For surgery of this magnitude, Stanford Medical Center or the Texas Heart Institute were considered, adding to my anxiety. A trip to an unfamiliar city on top of the health concerns?

I made to-do lists: telling our adult sons, informing other family and friends, settling business details, and the unmentionable "getting things in order."

Getting things in order claimed our attention for a while. But we talked. And talked. And we came to a sense of peace about the reality of life and its eventual consequence. "I've had a good life," my husband said, then amended, "*we've* had a good life." We became more appreciative of small pleasures and indulged in them for each other. We more openly thanked God for His care for us through the years.

> **The eternal God is your refuge, and underneath are the everlasting arms.**
>
> —DEUTERONOMY 33:27 (NIV)

There came the flurry of hurry-up-and-wait. After all the talk of the seriousness of the situation, appointments were difficult to schedule, and several were cancelled at the last moment. Doctors took vacations. Days became weeks, and still there was no definitive schedule. All the while the underlying tensions and what-ifs played hide-and-seek in both our minds.

Finally, a highly recommended surgeon who was located closer to us was able to accept us into his practice. I was inspired by the memorabilia and certification from Doctors Without Borders in his office. The doctor listened to our story and laughed off the "blood up to our ankles" comment. "I do several of these surgeries a week," he said, "sometimes in a day." Competence and confidence shone from his face, infusing my trembling heart with reassurance. Decisions were made.

> So do not fear, for
> I am with you; do
> not be dismayed,
> for I am your God.
> I will strengthen you
> and help you; I will
> uphold you with my
> righteous right hand.
>
> —ISAIAH 41:10 (NIV)

Surgery was scheduled for several weeks later—then postponed just as we were packed and ready to go to the hospital. Hurry up and wait again.

Throughout this journey, I continued my daily Bible study, a practice I'd had for several years. Sometimes I was inspired by immersing myself in Scripture; other times the devotional time felt mechanical. Several evenings before the final surgery date, the daily reading took me to Deuteronomy, not always the easiest book to read. But there it was: "The eternal God is your refuge, and underneath are the everlasting arms" (Deuteronomy 33:27, NIV). It was underlined from a previous reading, but I had forgotten it. Like a flashing neon light, it became my homing signal through that storm.

Finally, the morning of the surgery arrived. The surgeon bustled into the room, exuding quiet energy. He pulled a chair to the bedside and began to draw on the sheet with a black marker. I could only wonder what the laundry workers would think. He identified the blobs he drew as the aneurysms, explaining the procedures he intended. Then, just as quickly, he was gone with an "I'll see you later" nod of his head.

My son and I were directed to a top floor waiting room, more spacious and private than the tiny, claustrophobic waiting room on the surgery floor. Time to settle in for the long wait. We were the only people there except for an occasional ambulatory patient on his way to the adjacent open-air deck. My son pulled out a book; it was *Jurassic Park*. Funny, the details one remembers. I don't remember what book I had, probably because I didn't actually read that day.

Finally, just as we were told the surgery was finished, our younger son arrived from out of town, and the three of us were escorted into the room where my husband lay. He looked as if he'd been beaten. Since it was abdominal surgery, I hadn't been prepared to see his face dark red, swollen, and puffy, or the nasal tube taped to his cheek. But I wept in relief. I finally admitted, if only to myself, that I'd truly felt he might die on the operating table. Where was my faith?

> **I am not ashamed, for I know whom I have believed, and I am convinced that He is able to protect what I have entrusted to Him until that day.**
>
> —2 TIMOTHY 1:12 (NASB)

The surgeon explained that they'd found a third aneurysm that didn't show up in the X-rays because it had been masked by something else. He'd made the decision to repair the two bulbous ones, but left the thoracic one because it was evenly distended, not likely to burst. He called my husband a "tough old bird." Ha! I knew that!

The 8-week recovery period was slow, but we endured and then treasured it as we spent time discovering one another again. We enjoyed conversations we hadn't had for years. We watched old movies and sitcoms on television. When he began to feel better, he walked the backyard, building his stamina. We had fun picking up lunches from restaurants we'd forgotten we liked. In the seventh week, we endured some depression when it seemed his recovery had plateaued. Yet, on the dawn of the eighth week, almost suddenly, the swollen, sausage-like scars were flat, my husband's energy returned, and hope was back. The prognosis was good!

In the 2 years that followed, we acknowledged that God had granted us the extra time together as a gift. One hot July morning, my husband woke up knowing that instead of getting ready for work, he needed to call for help. Paramedics were called. Emergency room doctors ascertained my husband was bleeding internally. That last aneurysm had blown. Instead of coming home with me, my husband went home with his eternal Father.

And those everlasting arms have held me ever since.

The vibrations on the
air are the breath of God
speaking to man's soul.
Music is the language
of God.

—Ludwig van Beethoven

CHAPTER 3

Speaking through Song

The Prize Is Later, the Praise Is Now

Angela Unruh

"Is everything OK?" I asked.

The sonographer sat tight-lipped as she adjusted the monitor away from me. "You'll need to talk to the doctor."

That's when I knew that something was wrong with my unborn baby.

After another squirt of warm gel over my belly and a quick scan of the screen, my obstetrician transferred me to a group of perinatal doctors for immediate examination.

The specialist spoke gravely. "There's little chance that your baby will live."

My three-year-old, who had come to "see the baby on TV," handed me tissues one by one as I took in the news. My water had broken at 18 weeks. Only one doctor believed that my baby could be saved.

A tightrope walk of bedrest, careful monitoring, and daily check-ins would allow me to go home. Our neighbors and family members cared for our toddler. One night, I woke up with the sticky warmth of bright-red blood surrounding my body. My husband stood with a white face as the doctor told him over the phone that the baby was probably no longer alive.

"Your wife needs to get to the hospital immediately," she said. "Her life is in danger."

But on the way to the hospital, I felt movement. My little one was still living! Sure enough, when a nurse connected me to a monitor, the steady sound of heart tones filled the room.

My doctor's voice reverberated as nurses filled my veins with fluids. "You're staying here."

She didn't have to convince me. I was a pediatric nurse, and I knew it had been a close call to lose so much blood. How the baby was still alive, nobody knew. He was only about a pound, and he had survived a few weeks in my womb without fluid around him. Now this.

While fingers of the morning sun tickled the recesses of my hospital room, I sat resolved. *I can handle this. I have only one goal— to help my baby live until he is strong enough to be born.* But when night came, and the lights went out, I realized how alone we were. A constellation of monitor lights shone red and blue through the darkness. The tiny one wriggled now and then, a hard knot in my abdomen, without the usual bounce of a big, round belly. *I wish I could tell him everything's all right*, I thought. *I wish I could tell myself it's all right.* I flipped on the overhead light and reached for my Bible.

> "Our Father, which art in heaven, Hallowed be thy name. . . ."
>
> —MATTHEW 6:9 (KJV)

Psalm 139 comforted me with its reassurance that we are knit together in our mother's wombs—and that even the darkness is like light to God. Wiping tears from the page, I scribbled a reminder on a piece of paper and began praying.

"Dear Lord," I said, "after the news I've gotten about this situation, I know that You might be preparing me for a lifetime of mothering this child, but on the other hand, You may choose to take him."

My fear and loneliness faded as I talked to the Lord about the one thing in my life that hadn't changed—Himself. He was still my Creator. He was still my Father, and He was still the Savior. I turned off the light again and settled under the stiff cotton covers. My little lump of baby shifted. He probably hadn't heard a word of my whispered prayers to God. It seemed unfair for him to miss experiencing the communion of this communication.

He'd hear singing.

And so, hoping that both the Lord and the child would hear my voice, I began singing the traditional Lord's Prayer:

Our Father, which art in heaven, hallowed be thy name.
Thy kingdom come.
Thy will be done,
On earth, as it is in heaven.
Give us this day, our daily bread.
And forgive us our debts as we forgive our debtors.
And lead us not into temptation, but deliver us from evil.
For Thine is the kingdom, and the power, and the glory forever.
Amen.

A stillness descended despite the blinking lights, and I slept.

The next morning, there lay the scrawled note on the bedside table from the previous night's prayer. It said: "Look to God, and praise Him with me now, that He may know that we praise Him not only for our circumstances but for who He is." These words became a manifesto for me. I taped the reminder over my bed as a silent testimony: God would get the glory no matter what happened.

On my first day there, one of the specialists arrived and questioned why my doctor had ordered more interventions when this was a terminal situation.

Later, another perinatologist came in, sat on my bed, and patted me on the leg. "You can be home by tonight, and this whole thing can be over with."

I knew what she meant. But my usual compliance and desire to please had disappeared.

When my regular obstetrician heard about the pressure from the perinatologists, she agreed to manage my care herself. We had nothing to lose. Careful monitoring would minimize my risk. As long as the baby was still alive and I avoided infection, I would remain on complete bedrest until there was a possibility that the baby could survive being born.

> **Even the darkness will not be dark to you; the night will shine like the day, for darkness is as light to you. For you created my inmost being; you knit me together in my mother's womb.**
>
> —PSALM 139:12–13 (NIV)

Days went by. Every morning, the *kush, kush, kush* of the baby's heart and a reminder to keep praising God. Every day, a stream of kind visitors, and a compassionate corps of professional nurses accompanying an unflappable doctor. Every night, the blinking monitor lights. Then a prayer song lifted to God from two tremulous, dependent, intertwined humans.

Now and then, my husband and son stayed for an overnight visit—bringing two more little feet to shove into my ribs. We sang the Lord's Prayer together before we went to sleep. As time passed, the baby grew, and our hope grew.

In the middle of my complex medical case, a run-of-the-mill stomach virus wreaked havoc. Dehydrated and retching, I started feeling contractions. After singing the prayer that night, I stayed awake. It was only a matter of time until this little guy made his entrance.

> **My flesh and my heart may fail, but God is the strength of my heart and my portion forever.**
>
> —PSALM 73:26 (NIV)

The room glowed with sunlight as Mark arrived at high noon the next day, surprising us with a strong cry. All 2½ pounds of him and the top of his moist little head pressed against my cheek. All those nights. All those prayers. And now, day. God had brought us through both darkness and light with His steadfast love.

A triumphant neonatal team whisked our baby away by ambulance to our city's pediatric hospital. My husband stayed with me that night and we prayed together before a much-needed sleep.

Suddenly, a phone call pierced the quiet of a monitor-free room. Mark was fighting for his life. We implored the hospital to discharge me, but I had to stay under observation. My husband hugged me and left for the children's hospital. My knees and ankles creaked and buckled after weeks of complete bedrest, but I hobbled, pacing, begging the Lord to save my child after bringing us so far.

Whispered cries and tears filled my room that night—much different than the peaceful song, yet I was confident that God still heard. Darkness had returned, but God was still there.

I was released to visit Mark in the pediatric hospital the next day. His neonatologist told us that our baby's lungs were underdeveloped, and we would be in for a long battle. I knew Mark was a miracle from God. But I was so tired. How much longer could I hold on? Had God truly been guiding this medical misadventure?

Back home, I wondered how many days we had been in this fight. I studied my calendar, and my eyes widened as I calculated the days I'd been hospitalized. Forty days and forty nights. Just as God had led and blessed His people for forty days and nights before, He had put His "timestamp" on our trial in the hospital. Somehow, this realization renewed my faith that He had been guiding our journey from long before the crisis and would be for many days to come.

"Oh God," I prayed, "How could I ever doubt your unfailing love? You were there all along. Your hands held me. You knit my son in my womb. Thank You for where You've brought us. And Lord, thank You for who You are."

God brought us to the goal. Mark lived through the trials of that first year, and the Lord has brought him through many years since—a testimony that God's glory is the ultimate prize of our praise.

Blessed Assurances

Kathleen Stauffer

I was hopeful! I had encouraged my husband, David, to say "yes" to his brother's invitation to attend a Christian convention in Indianapolis, and he had agreed—reluctantly, because he didn't share my deep faith in God. We filled our station wagon with a backpack for each of our four children and headed out on the 500-mile trip.

I had a copy of the traditional hymn "Blessed Assurance" on my lap. We had sung the song recently in church. It kept tugging on my thoughts, and I wanted to commit it to memory so I could sing it without the lyrics in front of me. The words—*foretaste of glory divine, heir of salvation, purchase of God, born of His Spirit, washed in His blood*—were weighty. The chorus was easy and familiar—*This is my story, this is my song, praising my Savior all the day long.* Why had I never been gripped by these verses before? I wanted it to be my story, my song—me praising my Savior all the day long!

I needed it.

* * *

As a child growing up in Midwest farmlands, I was blessed with parents who understood the importance of church attendance.

We never missed. Come spring planting, harvest, rain or snow, we made the 12-mile trip to church.

Sunday school started at four years old, and one of the first songs I learned was "Jesus Loves Me." But due to my hearing issues, I heard the lyrics as, *Jesus loves me this silo.* . . . We had two large silos on our farm that appeared to stretch to the heavens, so I chose not to question the use of *silo* in a Sunday school song. However, my mother picked up on what I was singing one day and asked for clarification. She chuckled and lovingly explained; I smiled and understood.

Hymns lived in my head and my heart throughout my childhood. At the time, contemporary music in churches was unconventional. The songs for each service were based on scripture and posted on a hymn board so we would know the sequence. When I think back, it seemed that the first anthem every Sunday morning was "Holy, Holy, Holy." If we were not awake by the time we arrived at church in our finery, our emotions were stirred by the spirit of this song as the choir and congregation belted it out with great joy. Surely the angels had to be looking down with admiration.

When I was in high school, Lent was a favorite season of mine. It evoked emotions of brokenness that for some reason I could connect with. My eyes were often full of tears when "Beneath the Cross of Jesus" and "The Old Rugged Cross" were sung by worshippers who understood the cost Jesus paid for us with His Crucifixion.

Later, as a mother of four, the song "I Was There to Hear Your Borning Cry" soothed and inspired me, but it also wrenched my heart as it reminded me that these precious ones of mine were only with me a short time. They would go on with their own lives, and I would have to trust God with their protection and spiritual journeys.

But in the midst of all of this living—marriage, moving homes, having children, job changes, relationship struggles, older parent care—I at times became frustrated, even despairing. I started to feel like an extension of everyone else and their needs rather than a person in my own right, and bitterness took up residence in my heart. As time went on, I realized that when I woke each morning, the first word on my lips was a curse. It may not have been the worst of expletives—I grew up in a home where we did not even use the word *darn*! But it was a wake-up call to recognize my own poor attitude. What had happened to me? How had I gone from a girl with hymns in her heart to a woman with curses on her lips?

> **I am convinced that neither death nor life, neither angels nor demons, neither the present nor the future, nor any powers, neither height nor depth, nor anything else in all creation, will be able to separate us from the love of God that is in Christ Jesus our Lord.**
>
> **—ROMANS 8:38–39 (NIV)**

As time went on, I frequently asked God to forgive me for my frame of mind, but somehow the bad language kept slipping out. I decided to try to be intentional about what I was saying and replaced the usual expletive with *fudge*. I laughed as I said it.

At the same time, I knew it was not much of an improvement, and perhaps not an improvement at all. Even if the word was different, the mindset was the same.

Eventually *fudge* changed to *mercy*. I felt better about this step, but I knew there was still more work to do. I asked God to remove my grumpy early-morning words. Completely. *Can I just get up in the morning with a blank mind and a positive attitude, dear Lord?*

———— ◆ ————

Memorizing is difficult for me. The long trip to Indiana and back was only the beginning of my journey toward remembering the words of "Blessed Assurance." When I tried to sing the song without the lyrics in front of me, I would confuse one line with another, one word with another. Deciding that memory work was better done before I got too distracted by my day, I decided to tackle the task each morning upon waking. I set my sheet before me while eating breakfast to help me if I forgot a line or lost my place.

As time went on and I finally began to master the song, God surprised me with the answer to my prayers. The bad language vanished. Every morning, "Blessed Assurance" was on my lips as the sun slipped over the horizon. Weeks passed. I became more joyful—and my family was more joyful—due to my early-day positivity.

Then, another surprise. More praise songs began to come to me when I woke: "Morning Has Broken," "Beautiful Savior," "What a Friend We Have in Jesus," and more. All the songs I'd loved as a child, held somewhere in my memory during my growing-up years, came flowing back. Jesus opened the storehouse in my brain to a new song each day. One morning, after difficult family arguments the evening before, I woke with "Beneath the Cross of Jesus" and felt comforted, knowing that Jesus is mine, and there is a glory divine amidst our troubles if we live expectantly.

> "Hear this, you kings! Listen, you rulers! I, even I, will sing to the LORD; I will praise the LORD, the God of Israel, in song."
>
> —JUDGES 5:3 (NIV)

The morning songs have stayed with me to this day. Just recently, "Great Is Thy Faithfulness" filled my head as I drove my husband to Rochester, Minnesota, for medical appointments. Even though more tests would be needed to determine a diagnosis, the words encouraged me to trust in His promises and rely on His faithfulness even in the midst of uncertainty.

And it all happened because of a long road trip and a song that wouldn't let me go. I had hoped that my spouse would be changed by his experience, but maybe God had planned that trip for *me*. He works in everyone's lives in a unique way, and thanks to this experience, I know that He will always answer my prayers, even if I don't know when or how it will happen. What blessed assurance.

The Night Before Christmas

Diana Derringer

Late evening on Christmas Eve 2009, I stood in line at a large chain drugstore, my shoulders and eyelids drooping and my heart aching as I longed to focus on anything but the reason I was there. Instead of enjoying this usually festive night, I was worrying as my husband, Tim, lay in a rehabilitation hospital a few blocks away. A brain cancer survivor from 5 years before, it was his third hospitalization in the last 2 weeks.

Following a heart attack, stroke, and fall that resulted in a severe brain injury, Tim was not expected to live when hospital staff removed him from his respirator. Yet, when they gradually lowered his oxygen level and then removed it completely the day after those multiple health episodes, he breathed on his own, tracked motion and sound with his eyes, and squeezed our hands in response to questions. He was not expected to move his right side, walk, or speak. But he did. He was not expected to have any mental capabilities. But he did. He was not expected to remember anything at all. But he did. Bits and pieces of his lost memory slowly fell into place.

In spite of all the dire expectations, he sat up, talked with us, and made jokes 2 days after our medical scare. The hospital physician who had treated Tim during his first hospitalization said, "Well, I think we have us a miracle." He then turned to a nurse and said, "Get him in therapy now!" The cardiologist wrote in his medical notes, "Wow!" Staff in all three hospitals and the EMTs who initially responded referred to him as "the miracle man." Because of the speed of Tim's recovery, the cardiologist arranged for heart surgery in a larger out-of-town hospital, followed by in-patient rehabilitation in yet another city. I dodged shoppers and other travelers through the largest city in our state, plus another, smaller city, to reach the rehabilitation hospital where an ambulance had already transported him.

> **"The virgin will conceive and give birth to a son, and they will call him Immanuel" (which means "God with us").**
>
> —MATTHEW 1:23 (NIV)

Now, in that drugstore late on Christmas Eve, carols played. Last-minute bargain hunters paid for their picked-over, marked-down purchases. Lights twinkled. Clerks smiled, although I was sure most, if not all, wanted to be home with their families. Finally, I reached the front of the line, where a smiling pharmacist had dispensed package after package of remedies for colds, stomach bugs, high blood pressure, and a never-ending list of maladies that show no respect for holidays, regardless of how holy the night.

"May I help you?"

Although we had experienced miracle after miracle, those days of running on minimum sleep and maximum adrenaline, plus the impact of so much stress in such a brief time, suddenly hit. With that oh-so-kind question, my reserves crumbled and my blubbering began. When I finally pulled it together, in a shaky voice I explained that my husband required medication the hospital did not carry, and regulations prevented them from giving him the pills we brought from home. My voice calmed but the prescription shook as I handed it to him. He pretended not to notice. While he bustled about finding my husband's medication, I dabbed my eyes, blew my nose, and roamed nearby aisles to collect my thoughts and emotions.

Could he help me? Yes, with the medication my husband required. However, he had no prescription for my hurting heart, fears, stress, or exhaustion from days of dealing with the multiple unknowns that swirled through my brain.

Nevertheless, as I wandered aimlessly through the store, the words of those familiar carols filtering through the speakers spoke to me. "O Holy Night," "Silent Night," and "Joy to the World" filled my heart as well as my mind. Joy—yes, joy. That was what I needed. I had let circumstances replace the joy Jesus came to give and continues to give to all who accept it.

> **But I will sing of your strength, in the morning I will sing of your love; for you are my fortress, my refuge in times of trouble.**
>
> **—PSALM 59:16 (NIV)**

With that recognition, I mentally scrolled through our Christmas miracles. In no way did they match the miracle of that first Christmas. Nevertheless, I praised God for them and, without reserve, I embraced God's peace and presence as I opened my mind and heart to the joy of Jesus.

Our problems continued and our future remained uncertain. Yet, after I apologized to the clerk and thanked him for his service, I sang along with those songs of hope and promise as I walked out the door and drove the few blocks back to our hospital room. I rejoiced that Jesus had come and had sent the Holy Spirit to abide with us and comfort us through whatever challenges come our way.

I dropped off the medicine at the hospital nurse's station and hummed my way down the hall to our room. A tiny, crocheted Christmas tree and ceramic nativity scene from home greeted me. My husband, groggy after a busy day, roused long enough for us to read the Christmas story from Luke 2 as we do every year. When I reached verses 10 and 11, I felt as though the angel of the Lord spoke directly to me: "Do not be afraid. I bring you good news that will cause great joy for all the people. Today in the town of David a Savior has been born to you; he is the Messiah, the Lord" (NIV). Jesus, God with us, came not only for our eternal salvation but also for everlasting peace and presence. God was with us, had always been with us, and would never leave us. Whatever the future held, we could face it, secure in God's promises of a never-failing presence who walked with us through a near-death experience. Who held us close through multiple hospitalizations, surgery,

> "Be strong and courageous. Do not be afraid or terrified because of them, for the LORD your God goes with you; he will never leave you nor forsake you."
>
> —DEUTERONOMY 31:6 (NIV)

and therapy. Who loves us more than all the family and friends who supported us then and continue to support us now. Who gave me the tears needed to wash away the stress of those challenging days and who will provide all we need in the days ahead.

Secure in God's reassurance, I lowered the lights that night before Christmas and slept soundly in the abiding presence of Emmanuel, God with us.

Scripture, Song, and Sickness among the Shamrocks

Lisa Livezey

Despite my lack of Irish heritage, the first plane trip I ever took was to the Emerald Isle. Only 14 at the time, I felt a call to missionary work and heard of a church organizing a 2-week mission trip to Dublin, Ireland. Upon contacting them, I learned the team had been praying for a teenager to join their group!

The first team meeting was at a Philadelphia rowhome, an hour's drive from my house. My faithful mom drove me there and waited outside in her station wagon for the meeting's duration. (Thanks, Mom.) I climbed the steep steps, knocked at the door, and soon was ushered into a small living room where ten adults of varying ages offered warm words of welcome.

The team leader, Dan, began strumming his guitar and the group broke into hearty worship with many lifting their hands in praise. Some songs were familiar, some not, but all were scriptural. At prayer time, I sat quietly, feeling nervous. I didn't know any of these people. What was I thinking, going overseas to a foreign country with strangers? Fear gripped me as those around the circle continued in prayer. Seeking comfort, I opened the Bible and my eyes fell upon Psalm 34:1 (NIV):

"I will extol the Lord at all times; his praise will always be on my lips." I continued reading and came to verse 7: "The angel of the Lord encamps around those who fear him, and he delivers them." Just as I read those words, the person praying out loud quoted them verbatim! I felt stunned by the timing, but also comforted by what I could only understand as a sign from God that I would be safe among these people.

At meeting's end, I descended the steep steps, and climbed into Mom's station wagon. On the ride home I told her about the scripture moment. "The Lord spoke to you—He met you in the moment," she said matter-of-factly. I believed her. God somehow had caused the spontaneous prayer of a fellow team member to perfectly match the scripture I was reading—same version and all!

> **The angel of the Lord encamps around those who fear him, and he delivers them.**
>
> **—PSALM 34:7 (NIV)**

Three months later I sat looking out the narrow window of an Aer Lingus jet as we crossed the Atlantic Ocean above the clouds and landed in Shannon, Ireland. We drove cross-country to Dublin amidst lush rolling fields, made vibrant green by abundant rainfall.

The first morning in Dublin, our whole team traipsed down Grafton Street to the iconic Bewley's Café. Stationed along the lengthy table were three-tiered porcelain plate stands laden with scones, pastries, and other delicacies. We could choose any of them, and the final bill would account for it. I marveled how the servers could know exactly what had been taken. Selecting a scone scattered with raisins, I sliced it open and smothered it with clotted cream and jam. And the tea—oh, the authentically brewed tea, served in ceramic pots with hand-knit cozies and poured piping hot into our cups. My mouth waters at the memory.

Our mission team paired with a small Irish church that rented space adjacent to Trinity College in Dublin. Mornings began with Bible study, followed by a simple self-serve breakfast of cereal, bread, and fruit. I'll never forget the church member, full of Irish pluck, who daily expressed his disgust at the peanut butter we Americans loved to spread on our bread! After breakfast, Dan, our group leader, played his guitar and the vibrant singing began. My favorite song was from Isaiah 52:7, and it started like this:

> **How beautiful on the mountains are the feet of those who bring good news, who proclaim peace, who bring good tidings, who proclaim salvation, who say to Zion, "Your God reigns!"**
>
> **—ISAIAH 52:7 (NIV)**

How lovely on the mountains are the feet of them that bring good news, good news.

Announcing peace, proclaiming news of happiness.

Our God reigns, our God reigns, our God reigns!

My heart swelled at the words, bolstering my courage before we would head across the street to St. Stephen's Green at Trinity College and hand out gospel tracts to students. I had never tried outdoor evangelism, but my fellow team members were encouraging in both word and example. It rained intermittently, so we kept umbrellas handy at all times.

Afternoons offered free time to roam Dublin as colorful double-decker buses continuously rolled by. I shopped for souvenirs with Jane, a fellow teammate, and remember her excitedly pulling me inside the Laura Ashley shop to look at dresses.

Ten days into our 2-week trip, some team members fell ill with a 24-hour stomach bug. It spread rapidly through the group, both Americans and Irish. At first it seemed as though I would be spared, but 2 days later, while standing at the bank counter with passport in hand, exchanging dollars for pounds, the first wave of nausea hit. I struggled to complete the transaction as my head and stomach swirled. Green with nausea and feverish, I rushed outside, not even stopping to raise my umbrella in the pouring rain, hurrying past Bewley's with no thought of the sweets inside. I blindly stumbled, soaking wet, back to the church, where Jane compassionately saw me to my room, helped me change into dry clothes, and tucked me into bed.

A day later my head cleared, and it was then that I realized my passport was missing! Leader Dan accompanied me back to the bank. No passport. We walked along my route on Grafton Street knowing there was little chance of finding it. Dan took me to the American consulate in Dublin, where they arranged the paperwork necessary for my re-entry to the United States. Dan neither scolded nor chastised me for this inconvenience to his own time or team schedule but patiently showered me with kindness.

The next evening our flight touched down in Philadelphia. I waved goodbye to my missionary friends and climbed again into Mom's station wagon. While riding home, I told her all about my trip and how we stood on St. Stephen's Green at Trinity College and shared the good news that our God reigns! Looking back

GOD'S GIFT OF HEARING
— Kimberly Shumate —

SIT IN ANY grand music hall and listen to a professional symphony, and you'll hear something heavenly: a blending of different sounds and moods into a harmonious whole. The interweaving of ethereal flutes, romantic strings, extroverted horns, dramatic piano, crashing cymbals, and the thunder of a timpani drum. Beethoven, Bach, Stravinsky, Schubert, Mozart, and Rachmaninoff, they all heard it—the sound of splendid cooperation. The brilliance lies not only within each talented musician who plays their unique part, but also their collaboration in playing together. When God's children hear each other's unique voice and learn to complement it to create a greater unity, they glorify His entire work.

---

now, my real story seems less about evangelism and more about a kind mission team who rained sweet drops of Scripture, song, and support down upon a young teenage girl on her first-ever excursion abroad. And it might never have happened if a God-given sign hadn't encouraged me to trust in a group of strangers.

I leave you with lines from a favorite prayer known as "The Lorica of St. Patrick," patron saint of Ireland.

Christ be with me, Christ within me,
Christ behind me, Christ before me,
Christ beside me, Christ to win me,
Christ to comfort and restore me.

Amen.

Kvetching to
The Sound of Music
Anne Cohen

I've spent a lot of time kvetching to God and anyone who
will listen about the grave injustice of having two-fifths of
my grandchildren living twelve or thirteen time zones away,
depending on daylight saving time. I've lamented my losses to
long-suffering friends. I've complained in journals and in bitter
essays that should never be read by anyone. With tears streaming and fists clenched, I've railed at God, as if He didn't know,
about how I feel cheated that I'm missing the stuff of everyday
life that other grandmothers enjoy: tea parties and Candy Land
board games, puddle jumping and bedtime snuggling, cookie
baking and spoon licking. And I've failed, countless times, to be
appropriately thankful for FaceTime.

Then I've chided myself, sternly, about the wonderful
opportunity my daughter, her husband, and their little band have
been given. I've recalled my flippant retort to a neighbor—
years ago, when my children were choosing a university to
attend—when she wondered if they would move back to our
home area after they graduated.

"Oh, I have no delusions about that," I had quipped.
After all, I had followed my own parents' lead and intentionally planted seeds, lots of seeds, in my children's lives and

imaginations, hoping they would grow and produce fruits of bravery and curiosity. Hosting Japanese students in our home, taking my son and daughter to Ecuador to volunteer at a school when they were young teens, making sure their baby brains and vocal cords absorbed the sounds of Spanish so they could learn the language later, reading books about other lands, inviting missionaries and international students to our dinner table—these were the seeds. They sprouted and grew. And now I was paying the price.

> **You, Lord, are forgiving and good, abounding in love to all who call to you.**
>
> **—PSALM 86:5 (NIV)**

When my son-in-law told my then-pregnant daughter about an overseas engineering position with his company, she encouraged him to apply, buying in before he did. When they told me about it, their firstborn just days old, I said, "You'll get the job."

I was right. Six months later I stood weeping in the Atlanta airport as they headed toward airport security, that baby held snugly against her mother's chest, the two of them wrapped together with a sling.

Almost 6 years into their overseas career, I have cried at LAX, JFK, and HKG airports, among others. We have lived through Covid's closed borders and travel bans and l—o—n—g gaps between visits. My daughter has given birth to three more children who have birth certificates written in a language incomprehensible to me, as well as Consular Reports for Birth Abroad, proof of their U.S. citizenship—a document I had never even heard of. The three oldest children speak three languages: English with their father, Spanish with their mother—a linguist who wanted her children to be fluent in both English and Spanish—and the national language of the country where they live, one I can't name for security reasons. What sparkling pathways their brains must have!

On good days I remind myself they are following in my parents' footsteps. In 1967, when my dad was offered an overseas engineering job, Mom and Dad courageously moved their own little tribe from a mining town in Utah to another in Venezuela, south of the Orinoco River. There, my brothers and I learned Spanish, rode horses, played golf, and went on river trips in dugout canoes. On one of those adventures, we watched our dad kill and skin a 15-foot-long anaconda, shorter than it should have been, its missing tail likely a caiman's lunch somewhere along the way. We rode motorbikes and taught parrots to talk. I shouldn't begrudge my child and her children a gift I was given.

My most recent visit to the other side of the globe coincided with the arrival of, potentially, my last grandchild. I'd looked forward to this visit for months, bringing helping hands for tasks like doing laundry, escorting the children to and from school, washing dishes, and walking the dog. Spending time with my grandchildren and helping my postpartum daughter would fill my emotional tank. It wouldn't be glamorous, but I didn't want to be anywhere else.

I hadn't been in their home 24 hours when my heavily pregnant daughter asked if I wouldn't mind babysitting the children so she and her husband could have one last date as parents of three. *The Sound of Music* was being performed at a magnificent, newly opened theater center in a neighboring city. Her husband, through a work connection, had been offered two free tickets.

"Go! Of course. Go!" We both love this musical, and the only time we had seen it live, my daughter was in middle school.

Over breakfast the next morning, the city buzzing fourteen stories below, I learned more about the production. During intermission, my daughter and her husband had talked to two women who turned out to be stage moms, traveling with their children, who were in the cast of the show. The young actors, along with the entire cast and crew, had auditioned, trained, and rehearsed in New York City, then loaded their costumes, props, and lives on planes and headed to the opposite side of the world for an amazing adventure.

> **Rejoice always, pray continually, give thanks in all circumstances; for this is God's will for you in Christ Jesus.**
>
> —1 THESSALONIANS 5:16–18 (NIV)

Then she said, "You should have heard the Mother Superior. What pipes! I'd go see it again."

"Could I take Chloe tonight?" I blurted. Chloe was the oldest—the same one I had watched her mother carry through the airport as a 6-month-old baby. Now she was just weeks shy of six years old, the only one of her siblings old enough to appreciate a musical.

That single question triggered a flurry of activity: texting my son-in-law; checking the show's website for ticket availability; messaging the driver who transports their family to and from all activities, delivering them from the difficulty of driving in a city where three million people are always going somewhere. Available tickets were in the stratosphere or on the third row.

"The third row," I said. Aside from my plane ticket, these seats were the best investment of the trip.

Chloe didn't wear a white dress with a blue satin sash, but she looked like a princess in a seafoam confection with a smocked white eyelet collar, an Easter dress I had sewn for her mother 30 years earlier. She sat still through the entire musical, enthralled. I enjoyed watching her as much as I enjoyed the show. She made me remember my own edge-of-the-seat enthusiasm when I first saw the movie, under the supervision of nuns in the 1960s in Utah. During intermission we looked down into the orchestra pit and talked to the musicians before being shooed back to our seats by an enthusiastic teenage usher taking his job seriously.

Do everything without grumbling or arguing.

—PHILIPPIANS 2:14 (NIV)

When the final curtain fell, Chloe turned to me with both disappointment and hope in her eyes.

"Es todo, Lita?" Is that all, Grandma?

"Si, mi amor." Yes, my love.

"No quiero que termine." I don't want it to end.

I didn't want it to end either, suddenly struck by the realization that this evening was a gift we had been given by the God who understands pain and loss and sacrifice. He had heard my grumbling complaints and had not held them against me. Instead, in His boundless lovingkindness, He gave me an unimaginable treasure, these precious musical, magical moments and memories to share with my granddaughter. She lives half a world away from New York's Broadway, which had already seemed far for me, a 12-hour drive from my own home. With my grandchildren so far away, I would never have dreamed I'd be the one to take Chloe to see her first Broadway show. But now I have that memory, a "drop of golden sun," a reminder to be thankful when I am tempted to start kvetching again.

Before you speak, it is
necessary for you to listen,
for God speaks in the
silence of the heart.

—Mother Teresa

CHAPTER 4

A Voice in Your Heart

The One Constant in a Time of Change

J. P. Robinson

Everyone was on board with my idea of a family vacation last July. It would be an awesome time to reconnect as a family and would give my kids their first exposure to the European continent. Vacation was fine. It was my choice of destination that shocked everyone.

"Iceland?" My wife, who was born in the Caribbean and thrives in a homeostatic house temperature of 80 degrees year-round, recoiled. "Why Iceland?" she asked as a look of horror slipped across her beautiful face.

Our kids and friends were equally puzzled. I'd never been to Iceland. Sure, I'd heard of its stunning landscapes, but, when I looked it up on Google Maps, my aquaphobic eyes could only see a small speck of land surrounded by a literal ocean of merciless water. "Why Iceland?" was the question I'd hear repeatedly over the next few months as we prepared for our trip to the land of fire and ice. My answer was a consistent, "I don't know."

What I did know was that this trip was no accident. A still, small voice inside my heart kept whispering that there was something I needed to learn. That there was an answer to an unknown question that I would only find on this volcanic island in the Arctic Circle. So I pushed past the news that a volcano was erupting on the Reykjanes Peninsula, just a few miles from our Airbnb, and went on vacation.

For days, nothing spiritually illuminating happened. We did everything tourists normally do—explored nature, ate incredible food, and took Instagram-worthy pictures at must-see attractions. But, on the second-to-last day of our trip, it happened.

I'd taken the family on a 4-mile hike and descended 400 feet into the heart of a dormant volcano. Now, on our way back, I climbed a hill overlooking a plain coated with fissured igneous rock. The gray boulders lay strewn about as though tossed randomly from some giant's hand. Ringing the vast plain were the dormant volcanoes that had been a pivotal force in shaping this land. And it was there, as I quietly prayed while soaking in this stunning landscape, that I understood.

Iceland is an island renowned for its beauty. Tourists come from all corners of the planet to bathe in its mineral-rich lagoons and experience its breathtaking, almost fantastical, landscape. But all of this beauty is formed through some of the most violent forces nature can produce. The savage eruptions of volcanoes offer fertile soil while forming new crusts of earth. The tearing apart of the North American and Eurasian tectonic plates produce sudden earthquakes while younger mountains are formed by their brutal collision. Heavy glaciers rip the rough edges off mountains while creating unforgettable rock formations. Volatile weather and months without sunlight test the resilience of its inhabitants. Iceland is a harsh land, a demanding land, shaped by forces that crush, shatter, tear—and renew.

In many ways, Iceland's geographic story mirrors how God interacts with His believing children. Scripture is filled with examples of godly men and women who faced overwhelming forces at great personal cost. They struggled with social injustice, emotional devastation, economic hardship, and spiritual prejudice, to name just a few of their challenges. We admire these heroes for their faith, but we often overlook the frailty of their humanity. We forget that, like Job, they were crushed by the devastating nature of their grief. Or, like Mary, they were sometimes shattered by the struggle to follow God's plan in a time when it was not understood even by those who claimed to know Him. These heroes were ordinary people whose lives became extraordinary due to the magnitude of the opposition they overcame.

> **Then He said, "Go out, and stand on the mountain before the LORD."**
>
> —1 KINGS 19:11 (NKJV)

Standing on that hill overlooking an Icelandic plain, I learned that God shapes His people through adversity. He uses tectonic shifts in life to transform our spiritual landscape and bring us to our very best in Him. The breaking is part of the renewal, an essential part of God's design process.

Like the plain that spread out before me, my personal landscape is littered with rocky points. At the time of this experience, I was still dealing with the scars of a multiyear battle with depression. Struggles against racism within and without the church, against the grief of losing loved ones despite my prayers, against social marginalization because of my faith, and against the paralyzing impact of my own doubts and fears were just a few of my challenges. For years I sought answers. But that day, I understood that the beauty of a faith-filled life emerges from the harsh shaping of forces more powerful than myself. I understood that life's challenges don't arise on their own—they remain under God's control, and He wields them to accomplish His own great design.

Had it not been for the forces of nature that shape the land of fire and ice, there would be little reason for anyone to visit Iceland. But God, the great Creator, uses these forces to craft a land whose beauty appeals to tourists from around the world. The same can be said of those whose stories are recorded in Scripture. Were it not for the opposition faced by biblical heroes, it would be difficult to draw inspiration from their lives. The lesson is true for us as well. Each day we all write a page of our life story. And the beauty of our story can only be seen in our response to the breaking.

Yet there is more at work than the power of the breaking. Through all the tectonic shifts of life, there is a constant: the faithful presence of Jesus, who remains unchanged yester-day, today, and forever. He is present through every season of change, working His will in and through those who choose to trust in Him even when their world burns.

During our trip, I said to my wife, "Everything is going so well. The kids are having a great time, and we feel so relaxed. It almost seems as though God is giving us bit of quiet to prepare us for something ahead." In hindsight, those words seem prophetic.

————— ◆ —————

I successfully pastored an independent church for 13 years. We'd weathered immense storms together during that time. We came through the horrors of the pandemic with no deaths. We'd even continued in our global impact mission by coordinating relief efforts in Poland for Ukrainian refugees fleeing the war. Our church was rock-solid and time-tested. Or so we thought.

Last July, as I shepherded my family through the airport for our return flight home, I had no idea that within 4 short months, my church would be dissolved for reasons beyond my control. Within a few weeks of my return, I was informed that financial constraints and declining post-pandemic membership made church operations unsustainable. It was a tectonic shift that spawned a metaphoric eruption of emotions as my children faced the loss of their church family and we dealt with unexpected spiritual redirection. But the pressure was compounded on myself and my wife as we dealt with the financial fallout from the sudden loss of income.

> ## "Shall we indeed accept good from God, and shall we not accept adversity?"
>
> —JOB 2:10 (NKJV)

In December, I preached my last sermon and closed the doors a final time. Since that day, my mind has often circulated back to that moment in Iceland where a still, small voice whispered in my heart that God is behind all the changes that occur in the life of His children. God doesn't always stop the unexpected. One phone call can reroute the course of an entire life. In our case, He chose not to work a miracle and keep our doors open. But He was still there, using this situation as part of His process.

Recognizing God's omniscient presence in the breaking allows us to stand like the biblical heroes of old and move past our humanity to draw the strength we need from His divinity. When we do this, like Job, we emerge with a better understanding of His works and are left speechless at the wonder of who He is. Like Mary, we see the miracle of God's promise made real in our life. And our own life is renewed because of it.

Trust Me for Speed

Najah Drakes

My life was a mess. A complete, hanging-on-by-a-rapidly-unraveling-thread mess. Within 7 years, my husband and I welcomed five sons. My father was diagnosed with dementia on top of his already declining health. One of my sons had surgery after multiple hospitalizations. Another was diagnosed as neurodivergent. I wrote my first book, and I accepted the most challenging position of my career.

Between calls with my father's doctors and performing in-depth financial analysis for my job, I was changing diapers, chasing two toddlers, and completing homework with a first grader while trying to be the best mom possible to an amazing, forever curious second grader.

My marital, mental, emotional, and physical health were crumbling, but to the outside world, I appeared to be building a dream life with my devoted husband, handsome family, and a successfully advancing career.

From a young age, I learned to master the art of plastering a smile on my face while silently corralling tears deep within, my wounds invisible to the naked eye. But as my responsibilities grew, I struggled to keep the facade from cracking. Juggling too many balls at once made it harder to hear God's voice, and eventually my actions reflected it.

I needed an escape from my responsibilities, the kind of break beyond what a pedicure, spa day, or typical vacation could provide. I needed a place where the demands of life couldn't follow me, where I could shut the proverbial door and quiet the noise. I sought refuge.

Little did I know that a place of respite was located only minutes from my home at the Monastery of the Holy Spirit. Thirty minutes away from the bustling metropolis of Atlanta, where bumper-to-bumper traffic commences before the break of day and almost 100 million travelers pass through the world's busiest airport, lives a commune of Trappist monks. On hundreds of acres of land, adjacent to a duck-filled lake, this sanctuary houses a little over two dozen monks committed to practicing silence as a way of connecting to God. They live a simplistic life, take a vow of celibacy, and wear long, belted robes. They grow their food, bake their bread, grow bonsai trees, and run a gift shop. But their primary responsibility is to pray.

> "Come to me, all you who are weary and burdened, and I will give you rest. Take my yoke upon you and learn from me, for I am gentle and humble in heart, and you will find rest for your souls."
>
> —MATTHEW 11:28–30 (NIV)

When I found out this hidden gem hosted retreats, I audibly thanked the Lord and called to schedule the earliest available appointment. The cheerful receptionist informed me the next available retreat was focused on the topic of boundaries. "I don't need help with those," I responded quickly. "I pretty much have those under control."

But my desperation and God's prompting quickly overruled my resistance. I informed the receptionist, "I'll take it," and secured my spot for the upcoming weekend.

Excited but uncertain, I checked in on a Friday evening and was directed down several maze-like hallways and a few flights of stairs to my room. Upon finding my room number, I was met by three doors. The door to my left led to my suitemate. The door directly in front of me led to our shared bathroom. And the door to the right led to my room.

I tentatively entered the place I'd call home for the next 2 days. It was modest, with just a bed, a nightstand, a clock, and a Bible, but I was quickly hugged by its coziness and satisfying silence. My cell phone tucked away in my car, I stepped into a weekend of no rings, pings, or dings. Notifications, requests, and demands were on pause.

Despite running away to serenity, my Type-A personality followed me to my retreat. I scoured over the itinerary several times, and although I knew all activities were optional, I squeezed in every inch of what the weekend had to offer.

At the crack of dawn on a Saturday, I stumbled down mysterious hallways and entered the quaint church with its dimmed lighting, sweeping walls, celestial arching ceilings, and gorgeous stained glass. I sat on a wooden pew for my first monastic prayer, facing more than a dozen monks, separated by a center aisle that hosted a podium and various sacraments. It felt formal yet inviting. A need for reverence overtook me.

I fumbled through the order of activities while glorious chanting filled every crevice of the space and my soul, the words and message flooding my lungs with peace and comfort. I marinated in each moment as a brief sermon came forth, solemn and impactful. At the end of the service, the church bells tolled and attendees were dismissed in an orderly fashion.

Words could barely capture the experience. All I knew was I would attend the remaining six prayer times, skipping only the one at 3 a.m. I finally sensed what my life had been missing: the intentional practice of connecting with God in silence, without making a request, without placing expectations, merely basking in a presence I was unknowingly desperate to receive. I had become accustomed to a life where I felt guilty about sitting back and receiving. Here, I could luxuriously bathe in living hymns, scripture, and silence without adornment.

There is a time for everything, and a season for every activity under the heavens . . . a time to tear and a time to mend, a time to be silent and a time to speak.

—ECCLESIASTES 3:1, 7 (NIV)

The next day, the sky was overcast, but I showed up radiant, like a full moon shining. I entered my first retreat workshop and quickly realized my understanding of boundaries was misguided. I immediately bought and devoured the book *Boundaries* by Henry Cloud and John Townsend, and discovered that boundaries are a fundamental gateway to the rest and connection I was missing. Over the next 24 hours, God showed up in the unexpected. Through words spoken and unspoken, the whispers and the shouts, He was there.

A group of about ten retreat participants and I ate, paced, slept, and contemplated in silence. Most of us had arrived with full lives, yet our spiritual and emotional fuel tanks registered empty. We quickly understood that in the slow silence God's whispers could be heard, acknowledged, and welcomed. In the silence, we learned that "noise can be violent," as one of the monks put it; that reading the Bible should be slow and intentional; and that prayer can be contemplative, comprising mostly listening and minimal speaking.

> "All this I have spoken while still with you. But the Advocate, the Holy Spirit, whom the Father will send in my name, will teach you all things and will remind you of everything I have said to you."
>
> —JOHN 14:25–26 (NIV)

On Sunday, my silence mission ended; my chapter with the monks closed. I bade farewell to the monastery and turned my car's ignition to return to the life that initially summoned me there.

As I entered a narrow two-lane road and gently accelerated toward home, something felt awry.

Surveying my dashboard, I glanced down at the display panel and swiftly discovered my speedometer was malfunctioning. The indicator was stubbornly stuck at zero, though I was clearly moving. My internal sirens began sounding the alarm, and panic ensued. Barely out of the monastery's driveway, my default response settings jumped into gear—crisis, panic, react.

GOD'S GIFT OF HEARING
— Terrie Todd —

ISAIAH 30:15 (NIV) says, "This is what the Sovereign LORD, the Holy One of Israel, says: 'In repentance and rest is your salvation, in quietness and trust is your strength, but you would have none of it.'" Too often, we refuse to listen to silence, filling our moments and hours with all manner of noise rather than quieting ourselves in God's presence. Yet silence is often where His voice is most easily heard, His presence most keenly felt, and where His children can most effectively grow in trust and strength.

Amid this internal hurricane, it was as if God Himself tapped me on the shoulder, trying to remind me of the lessons I had voraciously consumed in the safety of the monastery. It was as if He was saying, "My child, it is time to truly digest what you learned and walk out the lessons that I spoke so clearly to you in the silence."

As I gathered my bearings, my confidence slowly inclined—and my foot gradually added pressure to the accelerator. I felt an invisible passenger occupying the seat next to me. And in the silence I heard, "Trust *Me* for the speed."

Resting in the confirmation that I was not alone, I cautiously made my way home. Mile by mile, God silently conveyed His concluding message to me. "When you are lost in the noise of the wilderness, you can always escape to a silent place in Me—no driving required. Slow down. Seek Me. And you will find the sound of a shepherd always listening for a single voice amongst the multitudes."

As I arrived home safely, I reflected on the most important lesson I learned after 3 days with the monks: when I quiet the noise and purposefully enjoy the journey instead of rushing to my destination, I will always arrive on time, at the right speed, and in step with the One who is patiently waiting for me.

Tara's Gifts

Leanne Jackson

Mary is a longtime member of my church. Her daughter, Tara, has an unusual gift: God speaks to her through her dreams. She tells me that these dreams are premonitions, vivid pictures of future events, and sometimes instructions on what to do when certain events happen. "They can be unsettling," she said, "because I usually don't understand what the dreams mean until they come true." That was the case when she had the first in a series of three dreams about becoming an organ donor.

Tara knew she wanted to be a doctor by the time she was in middle school. While in medical school, preparing to become a family-practice physician, she saw people whose lives were changed after they received an organ from a living donor. Their stories inspired Tara, and she hoped to become a living donor herself.

Then came the dreams. In the first, Tara had died. "I went to a space like a room, but with no defined boundaries, similar to a cloud. Some other young adults were reviewing my life in a book or on a computer screen. As they went through the events of my life, they said things like, 'This was very good,' or 'You did that very well.' Then one paused and looked at me. 'You were supposed to donate a kidney. Why didn't you?'

"It wasn't phrased as an accusation, but when I realized that they were talking about a specific person who should have gotten my kidney, I was so ashamed. I asked, 'Can I go back and do it? Or was someone else able to donate a kidney to that person when I didn't?'

"'No,' came the answer. 'The person died.'"

She took a breath. "That just pierced me through the heart. I could tell the reviewers were disappointed *for* me, not *in* me, but I knew that I'd missed an important opportunity I was supposed to have taken."

It would be many years before she understood who the dream was about.

Mandeep grew up in India and moved to Indianapolis, where she was working in IT/web design. After moving to the US, she was diagnosed with lupus, an autoimmune disease that was destroying her kidneys. After receiving dialysis for a year, the doctors told her it was not working. Her only hope was a kidney transplant.

The most likely transplant match is a close relative, so Mandeep's brother and sister were tested. One was not a match and the other had damaged kidneys. The doctors told her that the next most likely match would be someone of the same race or ethnic background, which made a match in the US less likely for her. Still, she stayed hopeful.

Mandeep believes we all worship the same God. She likes to pray in different houses of worship, whether churches, mosques, or temples. While attending my Methodist church, she met our senior pastor after one Sunday service. She told him her story and her fears. He prayed with her, then shared in his weekly email to the congregation that someone in our church needed a kidney.

Mary, Tara's mother, read the pastor's email. She was tested but was not able to donate because of her age. Determined to help Mandeep, Mary called Tara to tell her about the kidney request.

"My first thought was, *I hope that lady finds a kidney. But I can't do it. I'm a divorced mom of two with a more-than-full-time job.* I started to say no, but then I heard God's voice in my mind: *This is meant for you.* I have to admit, I didn't think that I was likely to be a match anyhow, so I went to get tested."

But, to her surprise, she was a match. That was when she remembered her dream and the way she had felt when she missed her divinely appointed opportunity to be faithful. God had granted her a second chance!

Tara tried to contact Mandeep, but Mandeep had been out of town for several weeks and didn't get the messages. Nor had Mandeep heard anything from the transplant list, so she assumed that Mary's daughter wasn't a match.

> "Obey everything I have commanded you. And surely I am with you always, to the very end of the age."
>
> —MATTHEW 28:20 (NIV)

It was only when Mary invited Tara and her children to church to meet Mandeep that the two finally connected. Mandeep arrived late to the service, so when she joined them in the balcony, they only were able to wave in greeting.

Seeing Mandeep for the first time, Tara recalled her second dream about an organ transplant.

In the dream, Tara had gone with her mother to meet a potential recipient of her organ, an unnamed, dark-skinned female. Tara assumed the woman was Christian because she attended a Christian church. But as the recipient shared her personal beliefs about God, Tara realized the other woman was not Christian. That bothered her so much that Tara told the recipient she couldn't be her donor. Tara's mother, Mary, looked on, "mortified and dumbfounded," as Tara recalled.

> **A voice came out of the cloud, saying, "This is my Son, my Chosen; listen to him!"**
>
> —LUKE 9:35 (RSV)

Tara thought about the dream during the remainder of the service. Would the events come true again? If Mandeep wasn't actually a Christian, would Tara be able to go through with the transplant? Tara felt God nudging her, saying, *Wait. Listen to Me.*

After the service, Mary made introductions. When Tara told Mandeep about the match, Mandeep was ecstatic. As they talked more, Mandeep excitedly described her deep faith, and sent Tara a link to an interview with a Hindu mystic. Tara was confused. *Doesn't Mandeep attend this church?* And, just as in the dream, Tara started to wonder if she, as a Christian, was betraying God by giving a kidney to someone of a different faith.

Then she remembered another part of the dream: her mother's keen disappointment in her. She heard the Holy Spirit say, *Don't be afraid to give her your kidney. This is My will, that you demonstrate the love of Christ to this person. Don't be a noisy gong.* Tara knew this was referring to 1 Corinthians 13:1 (RSV): "If

I speak in the tongues of men and of angels, but have not love, I am a noisy gong or a clanging cymbal."

After more tests, the transplant surgery was scheduled for the morning of December 21. Tara and Mandeep and their families gathered in a waiting room of Indiana University Hospital. Everyone was happy and excited. Suddenly, Tara recognized the scene.

She'd seen it in her third dream about the organ transplant. In the dream, she could not handle the pressure she felt from all the onlookers. She panicked, ran out of the hospital, and the surgery was cancelled. She had let the recipient down.

But now, fully awake and aware, she had no urge to bolt. Rather, she felt that "God was there. The Holy Spirit was with me, and with us."

Tara's right kidney was transplanted into Mandeep. Their surgeon called it a

> **If I speak in the tongues of men and of angels, but have not love, I am a noisy gong or a clanging cymbal.**
>
> —1 CORINTHIANS 13:1 (RSV)

"Ferrari kidney" because it roared to life and "pinked up" right away, a sign that it was working well, and Mandeep's body had accepted it without a problem.

Tara was discharged on December 22, and she was back in our church balcony on Christmas Eve. When the senior pastor pointed her out, the congregation gave her a standing ovation!

Mandeep lived in a historic home with steep stairs that were difficult for her right after the surgery, so Tara invited her to stay that first week in Tara's guest room on her ground floor. Mandeep's sister and brother-in-law came from Boston to care for their sister and brought homemade Indian food for everyone. Mary bought groceries and helped out. On January 3, both families celebrated with a lunch buffet at an Indian restaurant near the hospital where the transplant had taken place.

Today, Tara and Mandeep are both healthy. They are close friends who both tell me that they feel like sisters. And they both thank God that Tara obeyed His voice and His Word.

Put Not Your Trust in Princes

Luann Tennant Coyne

The area around my office building was beautiful and serene. Lush green lawns. A grove of shade trees. A forest preserve out back—a wilderness of tall grass and trees and hiking paths that stretched as far as the eye could see. Usually when I climbed to the fourth floor to take in the view through the floor-to-ceiling glass windows, the beauty of God's world gave me a sense of calm and joy. But not today.

Overnight, everything had changed. My great job with a terrific company was in jeopardy.

I had always felt lucky to work at a world-renowned company. The salary was great, the benefits even better. I enjoyed my work as a technical writer, learning and writing about new technologies. My coworkers were friendly and supportive. The job was close to home, and we had found a wonderful and trustworthy babysitter nearby who my two preschool children loved.

But then my company began to struggle.

One day everyone received a letter from the company lawyers. The letter said that they were legally required to tell us that we might be laid off in 2 months—or we might not be.

It was the first time I had ever experienced anything like this. Not only was it a threat to my family's financial stability, but it also felt like a personal blow. I had always worked hard, producing positive results, eager to show my supervisors what a good employee I was. This letter was a cold reminder that no matter how hard I worked, I could be laid off by some force beyond my supervisor's control. I felt as if I had gone from being a valued employee to a number that could be deleted from some mysterious spreadsheet at any moment.

I thought at first that I could ignore the letter and keep on working as if it had never happened. But of course I couldn't. The uncertainty was the hardest part. I often found myself staring at my desk, trying to decide what to do. Should I start looking for a new job? I did not want to uproot my children unnecessarily, separating them from their beloved sitter. And maybe I would still have my job in 2 months after all. Maybe.

> **Do not put your trust in princes, in human beings, who cannot save.**
>
> —PSALM 146:3 (NIV)

One day the tension and uncertainty got to me. I stood up from my desk, climbed the stairs to the fourth floor, and began walking. I hardly saw the beauty of the landscape below as I stalked through the corridors, angry and upset.

As I walked, Psalm 146:3 sprang to mind: "Do not put your trust in princes, in human beings, who cannot save" (NIV). I thought bitterly that the warning was as true today as it had been centuries ago when the Psalms were written.

I poured out my anger and frustration to God. "How can I do this?" I raged. "How can I keep right on working, ignoring the fact that I might not have a job in 2 months? The Bible says to not put your trust in princes, and it is right! But how can

I function, how can I keep on working here, when I no longer can trust the company I work for?"

Then I got an answer from God, an answer that changed my life.

Clear as anything, I heard, in my mind, *Put your trust in Me.*

That was my answer. How could I continue to work for this untrustworthy company? I didn't need to. The answer unfolded swiftly in my mind: I would work for God instead. It was as real in my mind as the papers I had signed on my first day at this company. I called it my new contract. It was a contract with God.

I could trust God. I could trust in God's promise that he would always take care of me and my family. God's part of the contract with me was that He would make sure that there was always food for my family to eat, a roof over our heads, and work for my hands to do. There was no guarantee of what that roof would be. It might even be a homeless shelter. The work might be volunteer work. It might be something I had never even heard of. There was also no guarantee that we would keep our house, or I would keep this job. But what I felt in my heart during that conversation with God was a guarantee that He would take care of me and my family, whether I stayed at this company or whether I was laid off.

> **I can do all this through him who gives me strength.**
>
> —PHILIPPIANS 4:13 (NIV)
>
> ❧

My part of the contract was to work to the best of my ability for 40 hours a week and put the future and everything else into God's hands.

This newfound understanding that I had a contract with God restored me to peace and serenity. I was able to go back downstairs and focus. Throughout the long 2 months of waiting to hear the fate of my job, I stayed calm while I worked. That all-consuming anxiety about my job was gone. God would take care of His part; all I had to do was take care of mine.

I was not laid off when the 2 months were up, but the layoffs continued, year after year, as my company continued to struggle. The difference was that I was no longer torn apart by uncertainty and anxiety every time a layoff was announced. Whenever another round of layoffs started, I would remind myself, "Do not put your trust in princes." Then I would remind myself of God's contract with me. Whether or not I'd be laid off, I'd always be taken care of, because I no longer worked for that company—I worked for God.

> ## The LORD is my strength and my shield; my heart trusts in him, and he helps me.
>
> —PSALM 28:7 (NIV)

I learned a second important lesson in those difficult years. Before then, I had valued myself based on how I did in my job. I felt good about myself when I got praise from my supervisor or when I received a good performance review. I needed someone else to tell me that I was valuable and worthwhile. When I lost that feeling in the workplace, I was forced to look elsewhere.

As I began to live under this new contract from a loving God, I also began to learn that my self-worth comes not from what I do, but from who I am. I am the beloved daughter of a loving God who loves me unconditionally.

Once I could see myself in that way, the praise and recognition I got at work was far less important to me. Whether my company succeeded or floundered, whether I would stay there or be laid off—none of that mattered in terms of who I was. I was beloved by God.

I learned to love myself unconditionally, as God loves me. Always.

Anchored to Grace

Bobbi L. Graffunder

This was a huge mistake. Let's just get it over with.

Not ideal words to be thinking before boarding an ocean-bound ship. My 15-year-old daughter was excited to embark on her first cruise experience, but I was dreading the week ahead.

On paper, it had sounded perfect. This wasn't just any cruise—it was a Christian music event called Mercy Me at Sea, filled with musical performances and worship. I had been on a similar cruise before and loved it, so I hadn't hesitated to sign my daughter up for this event. But then I learned that unlike the previous cruise, where everyone had been there for the same event, on this trip the event attendees would be only a small portion of the passengers. I was worried about who else might be on board and what kind of activities my daughter might be exposed to. But it was too late for a refund, so here we were in Fort Lauderdale, boarding the ship.

If I was honest, though, that was only part of my negativity about the trip. Along with my luggage, I carried a full load of confusion, anger, and sadness almost 2,000 miles to get here. The past months had taken a toll on my mental and physical health, though I was beginning to realize that the heaviness inside had been building for years, maybe even my whole life. The darkness had lodged in a place so deep I couldn't reach it, and I had lost my faith that this cruise would help.

A few weeks earlier, a friend and I had been driving through the wintry roads of northern Wisconsin. The sweeping landscape was like a picture-perfect holiday card. Regal evergreens adorned in fluffy white garlands of snow flanked frosty meadows. Under a deep blue sky, frozen ice crystals reflected beams of sunlight. Winter can be a monotony of gray, but there are days when the snow sparkles with the radiance of a million diamonds. Today, the pristine scenery did not match the dark, ominous storm within me.

A number of small incidents were piling up emotionally, times when friends and family took advantage of me and I couldn't bring myself to speak up. My friend listened, then bravely stepped into my pain: "Were you raised in a home with shame-based parenting?"

> **For sin shall no longer be your master, because you are not under the law, but under grace.**
>
> —ROMANS 6:14 (NIV)

What an odd question. I fired off a quick and confident reply: "No. Definitely not. I never felt unwanted by my mom and dad." *It's not them,* I added mentally. *It's everyone else.*

My mind went back to the waffle maker. I'd loaned it to a friend from church and then forgot about it, even after they moved out of the area. A year later, I bumped into a mutual acquaintance at the grocery store. She told me she was getting a lot of use out of it. I was confused. "You have my waffle maker?"

"Yes," she replied. "When the Hanks moved, they left it behind, so I borrowed it."

I was so confused. *Who does that? Why didn't someone give it back to me? Why tell me about it at this point?* A familiar feeling washed over me. *I am not worth respecting. There is something bad about me that I deserve to be treated like this.* But I simply didn't know how to respond to the woman in front of me. Even later, when I directly asked her to return it, her response was, "We're using it."

Incidents like that were constant, and every one of them chipped away at my self-esteem and led me deeper into a bad emotional place. Even when I tried to say "no" or stand up for myself, the people around me just ignored me and kept taking advantage. The questions kept coming back: Am I a bad person? Why else would people think it was OK to act like this?

———◆———

December turned to January and a new year began. Two weeks later, I was miles away from home, preparing to board the cruise ship. Miles away in my mind from that conversation about shame.

After my daughter and I unpacked, we made our way to the top deck to watch the ship's departure from the harbor. My daughter's enthusiasm put a little wind in my sails as we moved toward the open sea. There was definitely no turning back now.

The first evening of the cruise featured a welcome-aboard concert by the band Mercy Me and then a speaker named John Lynch. We had never heard of him, but as he began his message, a seemingly random thought pierced my heart: *Anchor your soul to grace.*

Stunned by those words, tears began to well from my eyes, then became a constant stream as I listened to the speaker on stage. The words John shared described my current struggles perfectly. Words like *perfectionism* and *mask-wearing*; concepts such as *identity in Christ* and *trusting God*. Internal walls crumbled as I pressed into my seat, too overwhelmed to move even if I had wanted to.

This was my "Jonah moment." I had been running in the wrong direction, trying to figure out how to fix myself to stop the pain. But here, now, in the belly of this whale, God had my full attention. As John continued speaking, a truth was fully revealed. Though I had disregarded her, my friend had intuitively pointed me in the right direction in that car conversation weeks before. At the core of my struggle was a mountain of shame. That was the heart of John Lynch's message. Shame. And grace.

I was instantly humbled as I realized I was exactly where God wanted me to be.

> **God made him who had no sin to be sin for us, so that in him we might become the righteousness of God.**
>
> —2 CORINTHIANS 5:21 (NIV)

The eyes of my heart were opened to all of the ways I strived to please others. Caring and serving became a way of seeking acceptance. Giving and complying were ways to prove I was worth loving. I was convinced if I disappointed or failed, love and acceptance would disappear for good. But it wasn't my parents whose love and acceptance I was afraid of losing. It was God's.

It didn't take much to reinforce this misconception. I didn't need anyone to shame me, because I was very good at shaming myself. For as long as I could remember, I had struggled with all forms of failure. Even as a young child, I often held myself to higher standards than my parents and teachers did. I liked doing things well. I felt safe when the world around me was in harmony. As I grew up, I struggled with Bible verses that seemed to demand an even higher standard of perfection. Verses that said, "If you love me, keep my commands" (John 14:15, NIV) and "No one who is born of God will continue to sin" (1 John 3:9, NIV). At some point, I burdened my young heart with the belief that my imperfections separated me from God in real time.

> **For all have sinned and fall short of the glory of God, and all are justified freely by his grace through the redemption that came by Christ Jesus.**
>
> **—ROMANS 3:23–24 (NIV)**

Because I had come to faith as a child, I struggled with the reality that each and every one of my biggest mistakes, failures, and overt sins occurred after I had professed belief in Jesus. I had repeatedly recommitted to my intention to do better and regularly questioned the authenticity of my salvation.

No one taught me this—but no one taught me otherwise.

I never doubted my parents wanted me, but I highly doubted God did. So I did what came naturally: I focused on doing the right thing and making no mistakes. And if I failed? When I failed? Then I took responsibility and doubled down on doing better. Every day I strove to give more, do more, and be more to earn what I didn't think could be freely given. If something wasn't working, my motto was simply "Try Harder." I was wholly anchored to inner-perfectionism and people-pleasing. And I was drowning.

GOD'S GIFT OF SIGHT
— Eryn Lynum —

WHEN A CREATURE turns toward or away from light, it follows a part of God's design called phototaxis. Positive phototaxis is an instinct to move toward light, like moths buzzing around a lamp. Negative phototaxis, found in earthworms or pill bugs (often called roly-polys), causes an insect to turn away from light.

God designed humans with positive phototaxis in their hearts. In His original design, humans are drawn to light—goodness, beauty, and truth. While negative feelings often disrupt that design and cause us to move toward darkness, we can correct our course just by following our deepest inner pull toward the Source of all light.

Until the moment everything changed. The moment when God whispered, *Anchor your soul to grace,* and John Lynch pointed me to a new understanding of who I am in Christ. Coming on this cruise wasn't a mistake. It was a divine appointment. It was a gift.

Before we even got to dinner that first night, I understood I had lived my life trying to prove to God I was worthy of His acceptance. In a way, I was trying to reimburse Jesus for paying my debt instead of receiving what He freely gave. I allowed every failure—or perceived failure—to stand between me and God until I was completely caged in. Shame imprisoned me, but grace was the key that opened the door to freedom.

In the days, weeks, and months since that night, I continued to grow, learning to trust what I had heard. As I read the Bible through a lens of grace instead of shame, the grip loosened. When I failed, or even made an innocent mistake, I reminded myself being a Christian doesn't mean I won't ever sin. It means my sin doesn't define me. It means my sin doesn't disqualify me from God's love.

As winter snow melted and spring blossoms transformed into summer fruit, I did something I never thought I would do. I got a tattoo. Permanently inked on the top of my foot is the image of an anchor joined to the word *grace*. I chose that location because when I feel shame, my head drops, and my eyes focus downward. In those moments, I want to be reminded I don't have to live that way anymore. Anchored to grace, I can instead choose to trust who the Bible says I am: loved, accepted, redeemed, chosen, and free. After everything I have done *for* God, maybe trusting *in* God pleases Him most of all.

You Can't Rake the Snow

Tera Elness

It was the morning of my forty-ninth birthday.

Excited to hear how God would celebrate His girl, I bounced up the stairs like a kid on Christmas morning. God's special-day greeting, however, was not what I expected. It's not that I thought He would sing a resounding, off-key "Happy Birthday to You," strew confetti, make a cake with candles, or any of the other things that friends or family would do. But I wasn't expecting what I heard in my heart as I entered our living room: *My Daughter, you can't rake the snow.*

Huh? Excuse me, Lord? What?

That's when it hit me. See, I had been talking to God a *lot* in the months and months leading up to that day. I had lamented over this new stage I found myself in; this new season that included hot flashes and heart palpitations and migraines I had never experienced. I had talked to Him about the realization that I would soon be reaching the top of that proverbial hill and was worried about what it would look like when the time finally came to go over it. I was scared. Terrified, actually. I didn't want to go over that hill; I wanted to stay on *this* side, where birthdays are filled with bright colors and joy, not black and black and more black—not to mention all the age jokes and graveyard décor.

As I stood there in the middle of our living room, windows flanked on each side, I noticed that the view to my left was crisp autumn leaves falling, while the view to my right was a gentle snow dancing its way down to earth. God proceeded with His unique birthday greeting: *My Daughter, you are standing between two seasons, and you can't rake the snow. It is time to find a new way to live, a new way to do things in order to thrive, a new lifestyle to adopt in order to live your best life.*

I stood stunned, unable to move. But would this unwanted birthday greeting somehow end up being the very best gift of all?

For that day was November 12, 2019, and I would soon discover, along with the rest of the world, just how relevant God's birthday greeting was to me that morning, how vital it would soon be to find a new way to do things. The personalized gift God gave me that day would prove to be the gift that indeed kept on giving once the Covid pandemic hit. Within just a matter of months, Zoom meetings would replace face-to-face; take-out and delivery would become a delicacy; walks and hikes and trips to parks would suddenly become not only great workouts but also much-needed vacations; and finding new ways to carry out our normal routines would move from a that-sounds-like-fun desire to a we-have-no-choice need. Indeed, we could not rake the snow.

> **So Naomi returned from Moab accompanied by Ruth the Moabite, her daughter-in-law, arriving in Bethlehem as the barley harvest was beginning.**
>
> —RUTH 1:22 (NIV)

I've never forgotten that morning, that birthday with the greeting I never expected or wanted. The greeting I couldn't have possibly known how much I would need, in far more ways than one.

God was right. God always is. I couldn't rake the snow, any easier than I could shovel the rain. I couldn't continue doing things as I always had done, for my season had changed. So, from that moment on, I would heed God's advice and begin to find a new way to fully live in this new season.

Over the years since, I have thought a lot about that day, that birthday morning I'll never forget. I've thought about my friend Naomi. You may know her from the stories about her in the Bible, and if not, I'm sure you've heard of her far more famous daughter-in-law-turned-daughter, Ruth. You see, my friend Naomi once found herself standing between two seasons. I believe that God said those same words to His daughter Naomi, a woman in a foreign land with foreign gods who now found herself both widow and bereaved mama, a woman who had once felt full of life and now felt completely void of it. A woman with

> Now to him who is able to do immeasurably more than all we ask or imagine, according to his power that is at work within us, to him be the glory in the church and in Christ Jesus throughout all generations, for ever and ever! Amen.
>
> —EPHESIANS 3:20–21 (NIV)

nothing left, *except* one faithful daughter-in-law and one faithful God. And, as it turned out, that was enough. It sure was. Like me, Naomi realized she could not rake the snow; her season had changed. She would need to move on to her next season. She would need to go back to her homeland, back to where the bread had finally been returned after years and years of famine. She would need to be strong and courageous as a single woman making her way through rough mountainous terrain on her journey back home with her Moabite daughter-in-law in tow, a young woman she must now care and provide for; a woman for whom she was now responsible. *But it was time.* Time to return to her hometown, a place where the neighbors would surely be talking, and the gossip would surely be flying. Small towns haven't changed all that much. But because she could not rake the snow . . . she would go. She had to, for it was time to find a new way to live in this new season of her life. And she did. And so did I.

My friend Naomi would go on to add the role of Nana to her repertoire, a name she never thought she'd hear until her grandson Obed was born. And she would know without a doubt that the God who had spoken her life into existence all those years ago, the God who had sent her away full and returned her empty-handed, really *was* faithful, really *was* her Redeemer. A Redeemer who did exceedingly and abundantly more than she could have ever asked for or imagined. And I'm willing to bet, as she rocked that sweet baby, the baby she never thought her empty arms would hold, she nodded to her God above as she sang to him this song: "I *know* that my Redeemer lives, in each and *every season.*"

Dreaming of Germany

Katie R. Dale

"You want to go to Germany? And you have a psychiatrist?" The doubtful tone in the voice of the family medical representative reflected the disappointing reality I feared. My heart sank in my chest as I sat next to my active-duty Air Force husband, Chris.

"So, don't count on it?" I asked to clarify I had heard right.

"Really, I don't want to say never, but for many of the members in our program, especially those under the care of a psychiatrist, it's hard to support."

I needed to gently release any dreams of living abroad. I swallowed back the lump forming in my throat and took a deep breath.

The next duty station our family had selected was now unofficially deemed unrealistic. Theoretically speaking, because my husband was about to be deployed to Qatar for a year, our family could have our top choice of where we would live together after that. However, I had a history of psychiatric hospitalizations and had seen a psychiatrist to provide medi-cation. That meant we had to deal with the military's special dependent medical program requirements, which included having medical resources and supports in place in case of health emergencies. Locations that are farther from providers can be a liability for the military and families. Because of these rules, the chances of our family moving overseas were statistically low.

As I braved the next few months without my husband, I ensured all my special medical program forms were filled out as efficiently and thoroughly as possible. What was crucial to note was that I had remained stable on the same dosage of psych medications for the last 15 to 20 years and didn't require outpatient therapy. I knew that as long as I took my medications and carried out a well-rounded lifestyle, I was not a concern for the clinicians.

Around this time, I'd read a book by Charity Kayembe Virkler titled *Hearing God Through Your Dreams.* Following Virkler's revelatory teachings, I kept track of my dreams using the two-way journaling method, in which I wrote down what I experienced and then listened for what God said about it, writing that down as well. In my journal I documented at least three dreams concerning the move to Germany that year, including one with a line of enormous yellow duck statues stretching from New York to New Jersey. God was telling me to "get my ducks in a row." If it was to happen, I had to prepare, and so I did.

> **I pray that the eyes of your heart may be enlightened in order that you may know the hope to which he has called you, the riches of his glorious inheritance in his holy people.**
>
> **—EPHESIANS 1:18 (NIV)**

With a mustard seed of faith, we mustered the belief that approval by the higher-ups would come. We prayed with my daughter and husband on our video calls nightly, begging God for Germany. In March of 2023, all the forms were completed, and I submitted the required medical forms to Ramstein Air Base later in June. We waited through July's heat, August's lagging, and September's sagging.

Finally, on October 9, we heard back from Ramstein's Medical Readiness Officer. Their answer: "Family medicine does not prescribe these medications. Medical Readiness Officer for psychiatry does NOT recommend travel."

Once that initial denial reached us, we rallied prayers and I gathered more "ducks" in a row. I conducted further research and made some phone calls. Within the 6-day reconsideration window, I resubmitted for appeal with a letter from my former psychiatrist and a longer letter from myself explaining the context of my condition, as well as the available off-base resources.

> **"In the last days, God says, I will pour out my Spirit on all people. Your sons and daughters will prophesy, your young men will see visions, your old men will dream dreams."**
>
> —ACTS 2:17 (NIV)

While awaiting the second and final verdict, I dreamed that Chris took us to every office in the chain of command and the case was approved step by step. In the dream, the final point of contact was a general who had a reel of photos from my last 20 years, having researched me for my behaviors and history. I was amazed they had pictures and videos of me back in high school and college. Near the end of the dream, there was a huge reception. My mom was there, wondering what the final decision was. I told her, "Mom, no matter what it is, we glorify God!" The comedic part of the dream was that the general was persuaded to decide in my favor by my husband bribing him with a peanut butter cookie (Chris notoriously makes peanut butter cookies for just about every military function).

It took the official deciding chain of command another 7 weeks to give us their final answer. By December 1, we questioned where they were. If it was taking so long, they could at least kill our agony of anticipation with a short "no." Yet, the God-given dreams of duck statues and a persuasive peanut butter cookie were not in vain.

> # I will praise the LORD, who counsels me; even at night my heart instructs me.
>
> —PSALM 16:7 (NIV)

One morning, in my journal, I asked God "How much longer?"

A few hours later, my husband met me with an announcement.

"Well, you don't have to doubt God's voice anymore: Ramstein overturned their denial."

"What? We're going to Germany?" For a moment I couldn't believe it, and then the reality set in.

Holy hand claps, praise the Lord, and pass the antidepressant! It was official—we were moving to Germany.

Joking aside, I did praise the Lord, loudly and repeatedly. Never again will I doubt God's prophetic voice speaking to my heart. Since tuning in to my dreams and using Virkler's interpretation method, I've had more experiences of God speaking to me in dreams. I believe anyone can use these same techniques. Our spirits don't sleep; God's spirit dwells with ours and uses dreams to speak to us in the night. With this knowledge, my life is forever changed.

As I write this, we've moved to the beautiful country of Germany and have been here about 3 months. I've since met with my primary care physician, who has set up a plan to prescribe my medications at 6-month intervals. Every day I awake to village church bells chiming, lifting me from my dream-filled sleep, reminding me of God's good plans, faithful words, and constant presence. God made my dreams of Germany come true—ducks, peanut butter cookies, and all.

What Kind of Man Is This?

Juliette Alvey

I was newly married and sitting at the kitchen table alone—a kitchen in an apartment all the way across the country from my hometown. Although I was excited to be with my husband on this new adventure, I had never wanted to move so far away from my parents. Living across the country while my husband attended seminary was difficult enough, but the thought that we might never live near them again felt like too much to bear.

Feeling a bit lonely, I picked up my Bible and started reading. *Maybe God will give me some words of comfort,* I thought, *words that make me feel warm and fuzzy inside. That would be nice.*

But that was not what God had planned for me that day. Just like any good parent, our heavenly Father does not always tell us what we *want* to hear or what makes us feel comfortable. Sometimes He gives us a challenging word that we don't want to hear.

The story I came across that day was about Jesus calling individuals to follow Him. Many of them respond by saying what they need to do first before they come along (Matthew 8:18–22). It reminds me of what happens when I tell my children it's time to leave the house. Their response (nine times out of ten) is, "OK, Mom, I just need to [fill in the blank]." There is always something they "just" need to do before they will follow me out the door. And in their defense, most of the time these are reasonable tasks: putting on shoes, brushing their teeth, finishing a level on a video game (OK, not so much on that last one).

One of the disciples in this story says to Jesus, "Lord, first let me go and bury my father" (Matthew 8:21, NIV), but Jesus responds, "Follow me, and let the dead bury their own dead" (Matthew 8:22). Wow. Really, Jesus? This man's request to take care of his family seems reasonable, and if I'm being honest, Jesus's response seems pretty harsh.

After reading this section, I had a lot of questions for God: "Why wouldn't You let him take care of his family? Isn't family good? What about me? Will I be able to live near my Mom and Dad again someday? What is so bad about wanting to put family first?"

> **But Jesus told him, "Follow me, and let the dead bury their own dead."**
>
> —MATTHEW 8:22 (NIV)

God did not answer these questions, but His message to me was clear: *Seek Me first.*

It was one of those moments in my life where I had to wrestle with God's Word to me. Even though it was crystal clear that it was true and from Him, I didn't want to believe it. I whined and cried at Him, "Why, Lord?" I began to list my doubts and complaints; I mourned the thought that my husband's calling would always take me far away from my childhood home.

The wonderful thing about God is that He is such a loving Father. Even though He did not answer the why, He listened and held me in His arms.

As I struggled, I looked deeper into His Word. One of my favorite ways of interpreting Scripture is to look at the sections right before and right after a part I am wrestling with. It is amazing how that tends to bring clarity. In the section right before the one I had been reading in Matthew 8, Jesus comes into Peter's house and heals his mother-in-law, who is in bed with a fever, and she immediately gets up and begins waiting on Him. That evening many are brought to Him who are demon-possessed and "he drove out the spirits with a word and healed all the sick" (Matthew 8:16, NIV).

> **He touched her hand and the fever left her, and she got up and began to wait on him.**
>
> —MATTHEW 8:15 (NIV)

The section right after His harsh words is when He and His disciples get into a boat and meet a furious storm on the water. The waves are crashing over the boat, yet Jesus is sleeping. When His disciples cry out to Him, "Lord, save us! We're going to drown!" (Matthew 8:25, NIV) He rebukes the storm, and the wind and waves die down and are calm.

When Jesus calms the storm, it causes the disciples—who thought they knew who they were following—to exclaim, "What kind of man is this? Even the winds and waves obey him!" (Matthew 8:27, NIV). What kind of man, indeed. This is the kind of man who is unlike any other, one with power and authority. This is the kind of man who does not come into the world to be served, but to serve and become a ransom for many. This is the kind of man who may ask His followers to

GOD'S GIFT OF TASTE
— Linda L. Kruschke —

MELT-IN-YOUR-MOUTH CHOCOLATE IS derived from the cacao bean, but the bean itself has a strong bitter taste. To create the delectable chocolate products that people the world over love requires hard work and added ingredients, like sugar and cream.

Sometimes the Word of God can seem bitter and hard to understand. But if one studies it diligently and seeks the counsel of the Holy Spirit, the deliciousness of His Word tastes sweet in the mouth and melts the hardest of hearts.

---

do difficult things, but who does not ask them to suffer in any way that He has not already suffered. As we see in these stories, Jesus has power over sickness, the devil, and death, but He does not just make them vanish into thin air; He takes them on himself when He goes to the cross. And then He rises victorious from the grave.

What kind of man is this? The kind that would not ask me to follow Him to places He hasn't already been or without a purpose. Through these stories of Jesus's power over the world, I am reminded that He is not an obstacle keeping me from getting what I want; He is the one through whom all good things come. He is the kind of Savior and Friend who will lead me to places that are better than what I would ever choose for myself—even if I don't understand the why just yet.

Each one of us is an outlet
to God and an inlet to God.

—Ernest Holmes

CHAPTER 5

When God Speaks through Others

An Opposite Word

Betty A. Rodgers-Kulich

Several years ago, I received a call after a routine mammogram. A suspicious mass of cells had been found in one of my images. I needed immediate answers. What did that mean? Was it cancer? But the individual scheduling the procedures didn't know—I would need in-depth ultrasound and biopsy at the hospital to know for sure. The earliest appointment was a month away.

Every day of waiting intensified my anxiety. The thought that I had cancer was never out of my mind. I tried to refocus my thoughts or distract myself with work. Sometimes it worked, and I would have a temporary reprieve from the frightening thoughts. But then, without warning, they would spring to the forefront, demanding attention. My anxious mind created images of my body scarred by mastectomy, the difficult and unknown consequences of chemo treatments, and the looming specter of premature death. The statistics I had read came back to haunt me. Every 20 seconds, blood goes to all parts of your body. That meant that in the month I had to wait to see the doctors for the ultrasound and biopsy, those cancer cells would circle my body more than 129,000 times. Every beat of my heart was increasing my risk and allowing the possibility that some other part of my body, not just my breast, was going to be overtaken with cancer.

How could the doctors make me wait a month? Didn't they care? With each passing day, I felt my chances of survival were retreating.

As Christians, my husband and I believed that God can heal people, as the Bible tells us in many places. We prayed together and read scriptures about healing, desperate for God to do something.

I read stories from other sources about people being healed from cancer, but I couldn't find the faith to believe that would happen for me. I remembered people I'd known who appeared much stronger in their faith than me and who had prayed for healing that had not come. Why would I think it would come for me? I found myself doubting that I would get my miracle. As I reflected on God's Word, I felt like the disciples who were out in a boat on the Sea of Galilee when a storm came up, who were afraid that their boat was about to sink, and yet Jesus slept. Their fear was my fear. Their declaration was mine. "Jesus, don't you care that I am perishing? Do something, Lord!"

> **In the same way, the Spirit helps us in our weakness. We do not know what we ought to pray for, but the Spirit himself intercedes for us through wordless groans.**
>
> **—ROMANS 8:26 (NIV)**

I realized that God had the power to do something about my circumstances—but would He? I had frequent thoughts about not being good enough. Did I have His intervention? What did I need to do to earn such a miracle? Would I have the faith and the trust to stand on His Words alone? Could

I really believe what His Word says when others who seemed strong in their faith had believed but not received their miracle?

All I could focus on was myself and the what-ifs. I had a choice to make. I knew what I should do according to His Word, but the fight to walk in faith moment by moment was more difficult than I had realized. My efforts were not enough, and the chaos in my mind raged on.

> **Then He arose and rebuked the wind, and said to the sea, "Peace, be still!" And the wind ceased and there was a great calm.**
>
> —MARK 4:39 (NKJV)

I needed Him to speak clearly so that I knew where all this was heading.

One Sunday morning before the upcoming procedures, I walked into church determined to win this battle over my negative thoughts. But I couldn't even enter into worship. I whispered as tears trickled down my face, "Where are you God? I can't do this without You." Closing my eyes, I bowed my head in defeat.

Suddenly, I felt a tap on my shoulder. A man who had been sitting on the other side of the church stood next to me, smiling. I knew him, but he had no knowledge of what I was going through. Through red, puffy eyes I looked at him blankly, wondering why he had come over to me.

"Excuse me, but God wants me to tell you something," the church member told me. "He says, 'It's not what it seems.' I hope that makes some sense to you."

I stared at his back as he turned and walked back to the other side of the church and took his seat. It was as if Jesus had arisen in my storm and rebuked it, saying "Peace, be still!" God had spoken.

The man didn't know what the message meant, but I did. God was not silent or unaware of my struggles. God was telling me that this mammogram was "false evidence that appeared real—F.E.A.R." Fear had grabbed hold of me, and now God wanted me to know that the upcoming biopsy would show that there wasn't any cancer and that everything was going to be OK.

Why had I been so fearful? Why had I not been able to tap into my faith? Rather than believe there could be many things that could cause the mammogram to read as it had, I immediately jumped to the verdict of cancer—and then let that F.E.A.R. cloud my faith.

> **The centurion answered and said, "Lord, I am not worthy that You should come under my roof. But only speak a word, and my servant will be healed."**
>
> **—MATTHEW 8:8 (NKJV)**

When the test results finally came back, the ultrasound and biopsy indeed showed there was nothing to be worried about. Cancer wasn't my fate.

That day I gained more than a clear future. I learned that God does come through for us, even in ways we would never imagine. He may wait until the last minute—as He did for me and the disciples—to bring peace to the storms, but He didn't fail them and He didn't fail me. His words to us can be trusted as truth.

Let It Go

A. J. Larry

A conversation with a family member years ago left me disheartened. What began as small and innocent chatter escalated into words of accusation that carried significant weight and had far-reaching effects. The other party retrieved a list from their car—I assumed they had brought it with them, planning to have this conversation—written on what appeared to be a short stack of perforated computer paper. Two fingers held the first sheet, allowing the other layers of the pages to unravel toward the ground as they delivered carefully crafted words to me one by one, detailing what appeared to be every misdeed I'd committed since childhood. In a sad attempt to stop the flow of words, I opened my mouth to speak, but I choked on my sobs. The air hung heavy between us as the fully unfurled list was regathered and tucked away. For years I carried the image of that moment with me, unable to make sense of it. Although we continued to see each other at family gatherings, our interactions were fewer and more awkward as I withdrew emotionally, harboring unforgiveness in my heart.

Time passed and that memory faded. Many years later, I found myself in the opposite position—grappling with the challenge of extending forgiveness to a fellow church leader who'd shown consistent disrespect toward me. Perhaps their position made it harder to accept that their subtle insults and sly jabs were aimed at me. I expected more, not just because this person was in a leadership position, but because we were both servants of God.

One Sunday, when I could no longer tolerate the subtle yet deliberate actions that pricked at my spirit and caused disharmony between us, I retrieved a pen and notepad from my purse and compiled a list of every one of their unrighteous acts. At first, I simply intended it as a memory aid, so I wouldn't forget what had happened. But as I thought about it, I decided that we needed to clear the air. I carefully tucked the paper away inside my purse and patiently waited for the opportunity to unburden my heart—having forgotten how it felt to be on the receiving end of such a list of grievances.

> **"Why do you look at the speck of sawdust in your brother's eye and pay no attention to the plank in your own eye?"**
>
> —MATTHEW 7:3 (NIV)

Finally, I decided to send a dinner invitation to the church leader who had caused me so much grief. When it was accepted, I was excited, knowing my moment had come. I felt that I had ignored the small things for too long, and they could escalate into significant issues if left unaddressed. I remembered the warning in Song of Solomon 2:15 (NIV): "Catch for us the foxes, the little foxes that ruin the vineyards." The "little foxes" serve as a metaphor for subtle issues that creep up almost unnoticed. Much like actual foxes, they can cause significant harm—digging, gnawing, chewing, and breaking things. If left untreated, they wreak havoc on our spiritual lives and relationships, causing gross and disproportionate damage. These "little foxes" were robbing me of peace, patience, kindness, and endurance—the very fruits of the Spirit that should define us as Christians. It felt like the right time for an intervention.

As I prepared for the dinner meeting the following week, I mentally put together my plan: simplicity, directness, and no room for diversion. Then came the divine intervention.

> **A person's wisdom yields patience; it is to one's glory to overlook an offense.**
>
> **—PROVERBS 19:11 (NIV)**

The Holy Spirit interrupted my thoughts, putting Matthew 6:14–15 (NIV) into my heart: "For if you forgive other people when they sin against you, your heavenly Father will also forgive you. But if you do not forgive others their sins, your Father will not forgive your sins." Suddenly, my mind shifted back through the years to the confrontation between me and my family member, a conversation that turned from friendly chitchat to something profound and weighty. For the first time, I felt their pain. Had I unintentionally hurt that person or made them feel small—perhaps in a way that felt as intentionally hostile to my family member as the church leader's behavior felt to me? It was a gut-wrenching realization. I now had a respect for my family member's position that I hadn't before.

Even still, I resisted the Lord's nudge to forgive, attempting to force the scriptures out of my mind. I continued preparing for the dinner meeting, but the word of God tugged away at my spirit, and the warmth of His love embraced me. *Let it go.*

Retrieving the list of frustrations from my purse, I read aloud each resentment, one by one, asking God to help me release them. When I finished praying, I discarded the note. My heart began to soften. Eventually, I decided to lean into God's embrace and let Him lead me to a place of humility and forgiveness.

But it was too late to cancel the dinner, so I forged ahead with my plans, uncertain how our conversation would unfold now that my heart was changed. As I reflected on the invitation I'd sent—an invitation that sounded more like a business proposition than a casual gathering—I was desperate for divine guidance and turned to God in prayer, asking Him to guide me to the right words and actions. As I arrived at the restaurant, I *still* wondered how God would reveal Himself to me.

And be ye kind one to another, tenderhearted, forgiving one another, even as God for Christ's sake hath forgiven you.

—EPHESIANS 4:32 (KJV)

Seated by the waiter at the corner table I'd requested when I made the reservations, I waited patiently, taking advantage of the moment to reevaluate the situation. It was clear that God was with me, and He expected my full obedience whether or not I fully accepted the understanding He was leading me toward.

Thirty minutes passed, and then an hour. It became clear that my guest wasn't coming. In my previous state of mind, before the Lord sent me that verse about forgiveness, I would have been furious, taking this as further evidence of the leader's disrespect for me. Now, I understood that God had intervened

GOD'S GIFT OF HEARING
— Kimberly Shumate —

"EVERYONE SHOULD BE quick to listen, slow to speak and slow to become angry" (James 1:19, NIV). Listening, really listening, is a virtue that requires our active participation. In the letter written by the Apostle James to the twelve tribes, he makes a point of warning new believers to practice this gift, and to couple it with a guarded tongue and an even temperament. To patiently hear someone out in a dispute, to quietly consider another's argument, and to keep the peace brings harmony to community and unity in the Spirit. Or, as James puts it in the next verse: "Human anger does not produce the righteousness that God desires." The fruit of listening is understanding, if not loving.

---

to stop the meeting, and I was relieved. I ordered myself dinner and continued to reflect on the situation.

As I examined my feelings and reactions, I discovered that my greatest disappointment wasn't the personal attacks against me, but the inconsistency between facts and testimony. As leaders, our character, conduct, and conversations matter; they leave lasting impressions. That realization prompted introspection: Was my character aligned with my actions and words? I recognized room for improvement.

I finished my meal and left the restaurant with a peaceful heart, for I had gained a valuable insight that day: To catch the little foxes, focus on bearing good fruit, maintaining consistency, and relying on the Holy Spirit.

The church leader never apologized for missing the dinner. Their behavior continued much as it had been until they moved away. I later learned that was God at work with them too: when the person returned to our church for a visit, they made a point of seeking me out with something better than an apology: "The Lord had me grow up."

Years later, I went to lunch with the family member who had confronted me. I wondered if that distant day still weighed on their heart. But when I carefully broached the subject, it proved to be only a vague memory for them. Most of the grievances had been relatively minor, little irritations that became smaller as they got farther away until they disappeared entirely. Our conversation flowed easily as we laughed and discussed sweet family matters.

A Boy, a Grandma, and an Arizona Sycamore

Lynne Hartke

Even though I was 5 years into this grandmother gig, I still didn't have it figured out. How did other women manage? In her lifetime, my mom had been the ultimate grandmother, keeping connected with thirteen grandchildren spread across the United States. She had made it look effortless, while I struggled. My grandchildren exhausted me, especially five-year-old Micah, a boundless bundle of energy.

I arrived in Tucson, Arizona, for a 3-day stay with our oldest son and his wife, along with Micah, three-year-old Madelyn, and one-year-old Benjamin. My morning began with a bean bag game in the backyard.

"Let's go to fifty, Grandma," suggested Micah as he tossed the first bean bag. The bag missed the cornhole board 6 feet away.

"How about ten?"

"OK."

But we counted to ten five times. The muscle in my right arm twinged on my back swing, ending round one of activity.

Round two consisted of blankets and pillows mounded in the entryway of Micah's bedroom for a hurdling competition, a one-boy show while I cheered as a captive spectator. Not to be ignored, Madelyn sat next to me with her doctor kit. She took my blood pressure with the toy equipment while Micah continuously jumped the pile.

For round three, Madelyn spun, her shoulder-length brown hair and pink blouse flaring around her, while Micah grabbed a small ball and tossed it across the carpet, kicking it against the closet door repeatedly until his mom yelled from downstairs, "No kicking that ball in the house!"

Micah grabbed a string for round four and raced back and forth across the playroom, knocking over his sister when she got in his way, which led to a timeout in his room under protest.

By lunchtime, I was drained. Wasn't this grandma role supposed to be carefree? Rewarding?

> **But blessed is the one who trusts in the LORD, whose confidence is in him. They will be like a tree planted by the water that sends out its roots by the stream.**
>
> **—JEREMIAH 17:7–8 (NIV)**

I felt disqualified. Lacking. I found myself eyeing the clock, counting the minutes until I could return to the quiet of my own home. The energy had been sucked right out of me, leaving me empty.

I didn't know what to do with this hollow space.

An Arizona tree held the answer.

———— ✦ ————

Earlier in February, my husband, Kevin, and I had driven to the Superstition Wilderness to hike the Rogers Trough trailhead.

We planned to hike 4 miles to a set of ruins before turning around.

When we arrived, the aftereffects of winter rain were on full display. The creek bed at Rogers Trough was alive with water. Not just standing water. Flowing water. Moving over boulders. Taking dried leaves for a spin. Painting pebbles with color. We crossed over the creek multiple times, balancing on slick rocks that occasionally shifted under our weight. We passed manzanita, juniper, and desert holly. Adding to the shades of green were the beaver-tail-shaped prickly pear and the Utah agave with its 14-inch serrated leaf blades.

"Is that a cottonwood tree?" I asked, pointing to an 80-foot giant towering over the creek bed up ahead.

"I don't think so," Kevin responded. "The trunk doesn't look right. And the leaves are too big."

I crunched my way through the five-pointed leaves that littered the riparian floor like rusty stars. The size of the leaves dwarfed my outstretched palm. "It's an Arizona sycamore!"

I had read about these trees but had never stood underneath the canopy of one before. The tree grows in riparian corridors, as the sycamore needs a permanent water supply to survive. Early Arizona pioneers had sought out sycamore trees when crossing the arid region. Even if moisture was not visible on the surface, settlers knew they could dig down and find life-giving water.

I leaned closer to the peeling white trunk for a better look, running my palm over the recorded history, the visual scarring. The mottled bark contained shades of beige, cream, and gray— an ever-changing mosaic of color.

Bark was not the only thing the tree had lost. The gnarled tree before me was a living testimony of its many seasons in the desert. Like other Arizona sycamores, this grandparent tree had cast off entire branches due to age, disease, or wind, leaving behind cavities for birds and other small mammals.

While we stood there, a bird poked its beak out from one such cavity, before darting back into the shadows, safe in its hollow space.

———◆———

As I sat on the couch in the living room, I thought of that grandparent tree and its cavities that provided shelter for living creatures. The sycamore's hollowed-out loss had become hollowed safety. Could the same be said of the places where I felt empty and inadequate?

The words from a verse about a tree planted by a stream that I had memorized as a child in Sunday school came to mind. Even in times of drought, the leaves were green, because of roots that went down deep to find water (Jeremiah 17:7–8).

> "**Whoever believes in me, as Scripture has said, rivers of living water will flow from within them.**"
>
> —JOHN 7:38 (NIV)

I knew I needed to be like an Arizona sycamore, stretching my roots down into deeper trust in God. As I contemplated the weight of responsibility I carried, I knew my mother must have also had her moments of inadequacy. She had turned to God in prayer. I needed to do the same. I took a moment and asked for help from Jesus, the source of life-giving water.

Later, after naptime, Micah joined me on the rug in front of the television to watch a cartoon. All elbows and knees, he had lost the fat rolls of his baby brother and the soft roundness of his toddler sister. He had been stretching for months now, reaching into the world of preschool activities and classroom friends.

Soon Micah climbed onto my lap—not to sit in a curled ball, but long and lean, his legs on my legs, his back against my chest, his head under my chin, like a hammock resting against my trunk. We swayed for a lazy 20 minutes, me with this container of unlimited energy as I rubbed his soft skin. We sat in hollowed safety.

But more than that. Hollowed safety had become hallowed.

We slipped into the holy as a young boy sat sheltered in trusted security. This active child trusted me enough to be the one with whom he could sit still. Not just as a young child, but as an image bearer of God. I was convinced Micah carried a little bit of God's loudness, an awesome task in a five-year-old body.

As the cartoon credits rolled, Micah wiggled out of his hammock position and scampered onto my shoulders. I cradled his climbing legs in my branches, protecting my glasses from his knobby knees.

He peered down at me. "Want to throw more bean bags, Grandma?"

A Pruned Perspective

Becky Hofstad

I sat in a circle with ten other women at church, just opening our eyes after praying for the morning ahead. Nearly ten times our number would arrive soon for Bible study.

One of the women asked, "Do you think we'll be here next week?" We all shared her apprehension. It was March 2020. Covid-19 was spreading, and uncertainty was swelling.

I stepped through the remainder of a routine Friday morning: I joined in singing opening hymns, read a short devotion, facilitated my discussion group, and took notes on a teaching from Luke 20. In the back of my mind, though, the news I was hearing about the virus kept swirling. *What will happen?*

After lunch, I soaked in the patchy mid-March sunshine as I sat cross-legged on the loveseat near my living room picture window awaiting the special live broadcast of a statement from the governor of Minnesota. His declaration: "Schools will remain open so that health-care workers are available to come to work."

What a relief. With my girls in school, I could continue writing. As the weekend unfolded, news notifications continued to appear on my phone: air travel restrictions and increases in hospital admissions. Sunday afternoon brought another announcement from the governor: public schools throughout the state would close.

The next morning, while others were stocking up on toilet paper, my elementary-school-age girls and I were at the public library. Every time they asked, "Can we get this one?" the answer was yes. We hauled several bags packed with books and DVDs to the checkout station. Midway through scanning, the message "limit reached" appeared. My library card was maxed out! We switched to my daughter's card and finished scanning. The library shut down the next day.

Over the next couple of weeks, everything came to a halt. We didn't dash off to church for the Lenten dinner before the Wednesday evening service. We didn't go swimming at the fitness center. I didn't have lunch plans with friends. Any writing I did happened in the early morning before my kids were awake. One of the things I missed most was climbing the stairs to the second floor at church to study God's Word on Friday mornings. I missed joining with other women to grow in my faith and, of course, to socialize.

We had no choice but to keep going as best we could despite the surreal circumstances. My husband worked from our basement, and my job became educating our children. I supplemented the meager materials supplied by their school with workbooks we had on hand and Internet resources.

I wish I could point to a faithful prayer practice and daily reading of God's Word as the supports that got me through those first months of isolation, but the task list each day crowded out my quiet time. My mind was unsettled. Without the accountability of a lesson to complete each week for Bible study, I floundered spiritually, and gradually maintaining stability for our family took priority over devotional time.

At the end of May, my anxiety spiked again as we watched the footage of George Floyd dying. It happened in our city.

The civil unrest that followed brought curfews, and on TV we watched public buildings burn only 7 miles away.

My husband and I knew it was time to do what we had put off: look for a church where our two adopted Black daughters weren't often the only people of color in the congregation. We needed to find a place where they could feel like insiders. The next Sunday, we cued up an online service at a nearby church that is Black-led and multiethnic. Our girls loved it. We didn't need to look any further.

In mid-August, 5 months into this strange life, school administrators announced that distance learning would continue for the entire 2020–2021 school year. I spent each day sitting between my daughters at a long table, working on our electronic devices. If I could go to bed knowing the schoolwork was done, the dishes were washed, and I had a meal plan for the next day, I felt a sense of accomplishment. As time passed, I, like the library card, was at capacity.

> **I am the true vine, and my Father is the gardener. He cuts off every branch in me that bears no fruit, while every branch that does bear fruit he prunes so that it will be even more fruitful.**
>
> —JOHN 15:1–2 (NIV)

Two weekly activities provided a reprieve: the solo trip I made to the grocery store and hopping online for my Bible study discussion group. I slipped away from my family to the upper level of our story-and-a-half house and hoped my kids didn't raise too much of a ruckus downstairs. I grieved the fact that I couldn't be more involved. In past years, I had read devotions and occasionally given the 40-minute teaching message to the larger group of women—most of whom were gathering again in person at our old church. Despite my scaled-back involvement, meeting virtually with twelve women in the same study I'd participated in for years was a lifeline.

By September of 2021, our new church was worshipping in person again, and our girls were back in school. It was time for me to recover. The Lord showed me, though, that if I was committed to participating in the same Friday morning Bible study I'd been so involved with at our old church, I wouldn't have the time to join something at our new church. So, by faith, I kept my eyes open for what came next.

Spending almost all of our time at home for 2 years had fueled our desire for a bigger house. I realized the "what came next" was sorting our belongings, packing boxes, moving to our new house, and getting our old one ready to put on the market. I only had about 6 weeks to recuperate from the intensity of the pandemic. When things settled down again, I was physically exhausted. I was also withering spiritually. I knew I needed to change something, but how? School would be out soon for the summer.

We found it difficult to meet people in our new church, because while the services were happening in person, the activities that would have helped us connect with other members of the congregation weren't back up and running yet. Instead, I kept in touch with friends from the Friday morning study at our old church.

While walking with Marisa, a friend from that group, she told me they would be studying the book of Revelation in the fall. I wouldn't have attempted to study this last book of the

Bible by myself, with its descriptions of beasts with multiple eyes, horns, and heads, but I longed to study it with a group. I prayed about it throughout the summer. I kept asking myself if I wanted to go back to my old Bible study group because it was comfortable. It was certainly easier than developing relationships with a whole new group of women. Our new church was offering a women's Bible study, but it was in the evening. A weekly commitment would take time away from family dinners, homework, and activities for our kids. I was concerned about being spread too thin.

As September approached, I was still waffling. The week before the study began, an email came from Marge, my discussion leader from many years ago. She shared that she planned to attend the Revelation study online. Four days later, our family ran into a couple from our old church at a restaurant. The wife, Sharon, had been the one who had the idea to start the Friday morning Bible study 20 years earlier. The next morning, my grocery cart crossed paths with Beth, who had shepherded our online group for the study of Acts.

> **Instruct the wise and they will be wiser still; teach the righteous and they will add to their learning.**
>
> **—PROVERBS 9:9 (NIV)**

"Hey, are you leading an online group this year?" I asked, hoping she'd say, "Yes, I am," and "Please join us." She did, and I did. Each week all the women in my discussion group would appear on my screen as I sat at my dining room table. The reassurances throughout Revelation of God's plan for all people bolstered me back into a vibrant life.

I attended the brunch at the end of our study year, seeing some of the ladies in person again for the first time in 3 years. Their hugs enveloped me. At the end of the morning, I filled out a registration card for the study of John the following fall, indicating that I wasn't sure whether I'd come in person or stay online. As I handed my card to Cheryl, she pressed, "It would really help in planning if you picked which option you'd like now." My snap decision to return in person was from the Holy Spirit. It was only much later that I realized the lesson behind it: being involved at two churches allowed me to have the best of both worlds, maintaining relationships with women I had studied the Bible with for years at our old church, while building relationships and gaining new perspectives in our new church.

The women in my old Bible study welcomed me gladly, and I was invited to be a discussion leader, but my girls' school schedule made that difficult. Instead, I agreed to be a sub for my group. A couple of months in, I asked Carole if I could give some devotions. She was relieved, as she had several trips planned that would take her away from our class. In late January, Cheryl asked if I would pray about giving a couple of the 40-minute teaching messages for our study the next year on the life of Moses. I prayed about it for a week, then said yes.

About 5 days later, a text came from Cheryl: *Could you teach in three weeks for Melanie? She is having surgery.* As I prepared the message on John 13, reading about Jesus washing His disciples' feet, I was immersed in His teaching about servanthood. Through preparing to teach this lesson, I heard Jesus's words as an encouragement—that sacrificial serving is what we are all called to in some way. I enjoyed presenting the lesson, trying to pinpoint the best way to bring Jesus's words to life. My languishing had turned lush; I felt like God was restoring the years the locusts had eaten.

Returning to my past level of involvement in an organized Bible study allowed me to see how my perspective had changed over 4 years. I now place a higher priority on spending time in God's Word understanding it is the source of nutrients I need daily. When my to-do list is long, I've learned that my best strategy is not to rush around, but to quiet down to meditate on God's sufficiency. By staying rooted in God's Word I am connected to the vine and better able to focus on what is most important. My natural inclination to raise my hand to meet needs in the community around me was naturally pruned away by the pandemic, when many activities halted. As I added commitments back into my life, I realized I was being more intentional about what I said "yes" to. For example, I discontinued volunteer work for my daughters' school writing grant applications. Instead, I sharpened my focus on my own spiritual development, and walking alongside others in their growth.

> **I will repay you for the years the locusts have eaten.**
>
> —JOEL 2:25 (NIV)

Of course, over this span of time, God never left me. It was I who drifted in and out of studying His Word as a regular practice. I no longer take for granted my ability to gather together with other women to discuss the deep meaning of all that is revealed to us in the Bible. It is the means our Creator has provided to know Him, learn His ways, and soak in the great love He has for each of His children. Studying God's Word isn't an activity. It's a necessity.

Faith Conquers Fear

Jeanne Roberson

My heart pounded so fast I thought it would burst through my chest as a wave of panic washed over me. My palms dampened with sweat. My body froze with fear. I visualized every horrific scenario imaginable happening in the houses around me, and nothing could bring me back to a normal state of mind.

I suffered from fears I didn't understand. Loud noises, neighbors arguing, a child screaming, or an animal rustling under my window at night could trigger an episode. Whenever gripped by this familiar terror, I always felt that I had to relocate myself to a safe place, even if there was no obvious physical danger to me. Staying with a friend was my best option, but no one was available tonight. So, I went to my next best choice: a hospital parking lot. Well-lit, with people coming and going, I knew I would feel safe there. For nights like this, I kept my car filled with gas and a pillow and blanket in the trunk. After finding a parking space in the hospital lot, I reclined my seat, pulled the blanket to my head, and hoped no one would notice me. I settled in and prayed that God would allow me a few hours of sleep.

I returned home at the first sign of daylight and looked for any indications of the violence I had imagined the night before. There were none. Not a shred of crime scene tape or a police car anywhere. Cautiously, I entered my house, moving slowly through each room, checking under the beds and opening closet doors, hoping no one was there waiting to hurt me. Everything was normal—everything except me.

These episodes occurred every night when I was alone in the house. The morning after, I would feel foolish, confused, and incapable of understanding why I believed an awful event had happened. *If anyone knew what was going on, they might think I was crazy.* I kept it to myself, with the exception of a few close friends. However, they could not comprehend the depth of my problem. They told me to have more faith, pray harder, meditate, and fast. But their advice only made me feel worse, because I did have faith. I prayed daily, begging God to take the oppression from me.

I arranged my life to accommodate the fear. Evening activities were out of the question. I wanted to be home and settled in before dark. I had a comfortable king-size bed, but I slept on the couch; I didn't feel safe without a second door in the room to escape if someone came through one entrance. My car keys and phone were always within arm's reach.

> **Fear not, for I am with you; be not dismayed, for I am your God. I will strengthen you, yes, I will help you, I will uphold you with My righteous right hand.**
>
> —ISAIAH 41:10 (NKJV)

When I finally sought help, the doctors told me I had a chemical imbalance and suffered from panic attacks and anxiety disorder. They suggested breathing techniques and tried a barrage of medications. Trilafon, Prozac, Wellbutrin, Valium, and Xanax were a few. I hated taking the drugs. None of them cured my fears. They made me sleepy and left me in a fog the next day.

Then one therapist asked me to list all the frightening events I could remember from my earliest childhood. As the list evolved, I began to recall incidents I had buried in the deepest core of my mind.

I am the oldest child and only girl of eight children. I grew up in poverty and lived in the projects. I suffered physical and emotional abuse at the hands of my parents and predators from the time I was three. I ran away from home at 14 years old, met a man, became pregnant, and married at 15. He became physically abusive shortly after our marriage, and I returned home to save my baby and myself.

> **I sought the LORD, and He heard me, and delivered me from all my fears.**
>
> —PSALM 34:4 (NKJV)

A month after my seventeenth birthday, I met a woman who groomed, manipulated, and trafficked me into the adult entertainment industry as an exotic dancer. I battled alcoholism, depression, and addiction. After 2 decades, I became sober and found my way out of that dark world. With God's help, I turned my life around. But the scars remained, resurfacing through my fears.

After sharing the list with my therapist, she determined that I had been misdiagnosed for many years—that I suffered from post-traumatic stress disorder (PTSD) caused by repeated traumatic events throughout my life. I didn't understand how that could be possible. I associated that disease with war and combat;

I had thought only military veterans experienced PTSD. But after my therapist began to describe the symptoms of PTSD, I recognized them in myself. Shocked, I wondered why I never related the trauma from my past to the fear that plagued me. Perhaps I had spent so much time in survival mode that the trauma seemed normal to me. Once I was out of that dark time, I never wanted to think of it again, so I buried it. Forever—or so I thought.

It was a relief to know I wasn't crazy. The screams I heard and the terror I felt were my own unaddressed cries for help. There were legitimate reasons for that intense fear, and the correct medication would help. Unfortunately, due to financial difficulties, I didn't have insurance to pay for the expensive medicines required to keep my disorder under control.

> **"Be strong and of good courage, do not fear nor be afraid of them; for the LORD your God, He is the One who goes with you. He will not leave you nor forsake you."**
>
> —DEUTERONOMY 31:6 (NKJV)

I continued to pray. I trusted God had a reason for allowing me to go through this and, in His time, would remove it. What I didn't foresee was that He would use a dear friend of mine who knew the Bible well to lead me to a place of healing.

When I confessed to my friend that I was sleeping in my car due to PTSD, she showed me great compassion. She told me to read the Psalms at night, to focus on reading Psalm 91 over and over, and try to stay in the house as long as possible.

GOD'S GIFT OF HEARING
— Tez Brooks —

THERE ARE THREE tiny bones in the human ear that aid in sound transmittal—the smallest bones in the body. As delicate and important as they are, the human ears never get periods of rest. Even while sleeping, the ears can never turn off. Although hearing continues when people sleep, the brain does not process sounds the same as when they're awake. Whether a person is conscious or not, softer noises still enter the ear but rarely wake them unless it's loud enough to alert the brain and startle the individual in case of danger. The exquisite mechanisms of God's design are truly without number.

I had heard Psalm 91 before, but when I began to read it at night, the words struck me anew. God as my refuge and fortress, whose wings cover me, whose truth shields me. "You shall not be afraid of the terror by night. . . . Because you have made the LORD, who is my refuge, even the Most High, your dwelling place, no evil shall befall you, nor shall any plague come near your dwelling; for He shall give His angels charge over you, to keep you in all your ways." (Psalm 91:5, 9–11, NKJV).

My friend told me that if I felt overwhelmed, I could go to her house and sleep, no matter the time. And I did. There were so many nights I showed up on her doorstep at some late hour, embarrassed that I couldn't get through the night.

Then something happened I didn't expect.

One morning, the sun crept through the blinds, and I woke with it shining on my face. My Bible lay beside me on the couch, still open. I had fallen asleep reading Psalm 91. What a wonderful feeling to wake up in my own house. I basked in the comfort of not having to get up and drive home.

Later that morning, I called my friend. She said she had been waiting for me, and when I didn't show up, she began to pray and continued to pray throughout the night. We celebrated my victory with prayers of gratitude.

I continued to have occasional episodes, but on most nights, I got through them without leaving the house. I visualized myself tucked in the corner of an enormous white feathered wing, safe and protected by God. I told myself that if God wanted to take me, He could do so at any time, so what did I have to fear? Psalm 91 gave me a vision of God's love for me and a promise that because I was faithful, He would protect me.

A Change in Perspective

Mindy Baker

During an epic family vacation out west, our family toured some of the region's most splendid sites. We marveled at the beauty of Zion National Park, the immensity of the Grand Canyon, and the stunning interior of the Antelope Canyon. Each place was a unique display of the artistic ability of our magnificent Creator. On the last day of our trip, we ventured to Sedona, Arizona, to Slide Rock State Park. It is a beautiful place where rushing water has cut its way through a canyon and formed natural waterslides. Tourists and families travel for miles to swim, splash, and slide down the waterslides.

We spent several hours riding the waterslides and traipsing over the rocky shallow areas, pausing to rest on large boulders, bask in the beauty of the area, and enjoy family time together. When we finally decided it was time to pack up and head home, my husband went ahead to the car to grab a camera so we could snap a few pictures before we left. The kids and I began carefully navigating our way back among the rocky terrain, laughing and chatting along the way.

About a mile from where we were parked, I suddenly caught my toe on a rock, tripped, and fell into the shallow water near one of the natural waterslides. I heard a loud crack as I went down, and instantly felt extreme pain in my ankle. My foot was dangling at an angle that left no doubt that I needed emergency help. My son ran to find my husband, and a stranger called the paramedics. Soon a small crowd gathered, while my two daughters tried to help me out of the water and onto a flat surface to rest. As I sat at the water's edge in the canyon awaiting my rescue, I tried to stay calm. *God, help me*, I prayed, over and over. In spite of the tremendous pain, a supernatural peace came over me.

Not too many minutes later, the medics arrived, strapped me to a stretcher, and carried me out of the canyon. After an ambulance ride to a hospital in Flagstaff, I found out that I had what is called a trimalleolar fracture, meaning that I had snapped all three bones in my ankle. I had to undergo an emergency procedure to straighten the bones.

> **Your steadfast love, O Lord, extends to the heavens, your faithfulness to the clouds.**
>
> —PSALM 36:5 (ESV)

The next day I had a more complex surgery to further repair the injury. I will never forget the take-charge EMTs, caring nursing staff, and skilled doctors who attended to my needs. I knew God had placed them there to help me, and I was grateful for their expertise.

Although we were scheduled to fly home the same evening of my surgery, after much consideration, we postponed our flight and stayed in Phoenix for three additional nights to give me time to recuperate.

Up until that point, we had been dealing with events moment by moment. It was only once we reached the hotel that the situation started to sink in: how the injury would affect my day-to-day routine, how long it would take me to recover, and the limitations I would have to deal with during that time. All my plans for the upcoming months had come to a screeching halt.

I began soul searching. And reading my Bible. Did I have enough faith to trust God even when life wasn't going the way I intended it to go?

Right away, God began to use Scripture to reassure me of His faithful and steadfast love even when my circumstances were not what I wanted. I turned to Lamentations 3:22–23 (ESV), "The steadfast love of the LORD never ceases; his mercies never come to an end; they are new every morning; great is your faithfulness," and Psalm 36:5 (ESV), "Your steadfast love, O LORD, extends to the heavens, your faithfulness to the clouds." He also gave me additional scriptures to remind me to depend on His strength and not my own. One special verse was from Psalm 105:4 (NIV): "Look to the LORD and his strength; seek his face always." Another one was from 2 Timothy 4:17 (NIV): "But the Lord stood by my side and gave me strength." Each precious verse I wrote down in my journal and read over and over, not just during the hotel stay, but also in the days and weeks that followed. I found that saying these verses aloud helped me to focus my mind on the truth instead of allowing negative emotions to control my thoughts.

> ## Look to the LORD and his strength; seek his face always.
>
> **—PSALM 105:4 (NIV)**

During the next few months, I faced many trials. I could not bear weight on the injured ankle for 6 weeks. And it was several months after that before I was walking without a boot or scooter. I am a teacher, and because of the severity of my injury, I was not able to start the school year with my students. Also, my husband had planned an overseas mission trip and had to be away for 3½ weeks of my recovery. The wife of one of his coworkers volunteered to come and stay with me to assist me. Over and over again I had to humble myself and be willing to receive help from others. I will be forever grateful to the many friends who ministered to me during this trial.

Despite the encouragement from family and friends, there were still many times during my recovery when I felt despair. On one such day, a close friend of mine texted me a YouTube video of a song she had been listening to frequently. One of the lines quoted in the song was from Zechariah 4:6 (NIV): "'Not by might, nor by power, but by my Spirit,' says the LORD Almighty." When I first listened to the song, tears formed in my eyes. I thought about how incapable I was of doing even the smallest task. Recovery was not going quickly, nor could it be hurried. I read the Scripture over and over, and I felt the Holy Spirit impressing on my heart, *I am at work using this situation for my purposes. Your healing will come, but it will* not *be by any strength you can muster on your own. Let the* Spirit of the Living God *minister to you in this moment and trust in Me.*

Through this experience I discovered the steadfast love and presence of the Savior when all hope seemed lost. I learned how to trust Him for the next step when I couldn't see how

> ## But the Lord stood at my side and gave me strength.
>
> —2 TIMOTHY 4:17 (NIV)
>
> ⚜

the problem would be solved. And every step of the way He met me, supplying what I needed at just the right time. Scripture ministered to me in a profound way, changing my heart and changing my perspective. Although my circumstances were different than I would have chosen, by placing my faith in Him and trusting in the promise of His Word, God gave me the ability to overcome seemingly impossible challenges.

Every happening, great
and small, is a parable
whereby God speaks to
us, and the art of life is
to get the message.

—Malcolm Muggeridge

CHAPTER 6

God Sends a Sign

I Have Heard Your Prayers

Mabelle Reamer

I can see! I realized when I opened my eyes after surgery. After two surgeons and 6 hours, the tumor that had been blocking the vision in my right eye for the past year had been removed.

As I lay on my hospital bed later that day, I thanked God the tumor was benign, and that the surgery had gone well with no complications. But I had weeks of recovery ahead of me.

Once I returned home, I found that my mind was foggy most of the time, I couldn't focus or take a lot of noise or bright lights, and I was in pain. To make matters worse, I now had double vision in the eye where the tumor had been, which gave me a nauseating "just-got-off-the-tilt-a-whirl" feeling and affected my balance. The doctors were hopeful this would right itself in time, although that wasn't the case for everyone.

Throughout the coming weeks, I prayed, as did many others, that God would bring healing. He graciously answered that prayer. The lack of focus lifted, and so did the pain. I felt almost normal again. But the double vision stayed with me. In the days ahead, the doctors prescribed a corrective lens for my glasses that took away the double vision. It was amazing to actually see normally again, and I thanked God for this gift that kept the nausea away and enabled me to drive and go back to work again.

But in my heart, I hoped that my vision would be completely restored. I continued to pray about the double vision

I had when I wasn't wearing the glasses. I knew God could heal me if that was in His plan for me. But what if His plan meant healing would be a while coming, or perhaps not in the way I hoped? What if my "old normal" never came back? What if His answer was "no," "not yet," or "not until heaven"?

I struggled with the possible long-term outcome of His answer. Sometimes I wondered if He even heard me. I knew I could function and learn to accept things as they were. But I longed to open my eyes without seeing two of everything.

Perhaps I shouldn't even ask Him to heal my eye, I thought. After all, I was grateful that I could see fine as long as I wore my glasses. As I prayed, I asked God to help me accept the fact that He may have another reason for not healing my eye the way I wanted. I knew, too, that He wanted me to trust Him no matter the outcome, knowing He would give me grace to live with the double vision if it never went away.

> **I have heard your prayer and seen your tears; I will heal you.**
>
> —2 KINGS 20:5 (NIV)

I remembered 2 Corinthians 12:9 (NIV), where Paul asked the Lord to take away his thorn in the flesh. Instead of taking it away, God promised him, "My grace is sufficient for you, for my power is made perfect in weakness." I knew He wanted me to realize that too.

Unfortunately, fear and doubt have been frequent companions of mine over the years. Now they often showed up in full force. I had to decide to either trust Him or not, even if my vision never changed. I hated that it often seemed like such a battle, one I too frequently lost.

One afternoon, I stopped by a local craft store, and a sign on a shelf stopped me in my tracks: "I have heard your prayers, and I will heal you."

The words took my breath away for a moment. I stood and looked at the sign.

At first, I didn't know what to think. I certainly didn't want to read something into the situation that wasn't true, but this seemed to be more than a coincidence. It was an ordinary sign, but the words at that place and time were not ordinary, considering my struggle to trust Him. That nagging question of whether He even heard my request had trickled through my mind more than once.

> **Before they call**
> **I will answer;**
> **while they are still**
> **speaking I will hear.**
>
> —ISAIAH 65:24 (NIV)

"God," I whispered, "are You trying to tell me something?"

Could something so simple really be from God?

I knew in that moment that this was a reminder for me that God heard my prayer. He knew about my struggle with faith over doubt and fear. Being the kind, faithful Father He is, He let me know in big, bold letters, on a literal sign He had to put right in front of my face, an acknowledgement that, "Yes, child, I heard you."

Not only did He hear me, but my eye would be healed. When? Next week? Next month? In a year? What if it didn't come until He took me home to heaven? I had no idea. I only knew it would be in God's time.

As the understanding sank in, I realized the greatest healing for me wouldn't be my eye, but the strengthening of my wobbly faith. He would hear and care for me, no matter what

GOD'S GIFT OF SIGHT
— Heidi Gaul —

A RAINBOW IS a dispersion of light reflected in water droplets, creating a prism of red, orange, yellow, green, cyan, blue, and violet. Whenever I see these elegant arches, I am reminded of God's message in Genesis 9:13 (NIV): I have set my rainbow in the clouds, and it will be the sign of the covenant between me and the earth.

A single rainbow made up of only seven colors can take our breath away. A double rainbow can leave us speechless. Yet the American Academy of Ophthalmology reports that the human eye senses an astounding ten million separate color tones. God, in His lavish generosity, has gifted us the myriad colors of all creation. The blessing—the miracle—of sight.

happened with my sight. He would be faithful no matter what I was facing, and He would always do what's best for me. Finally, my soul was at peace.

I will always remember the morning, many days later, when I woke up and the double vision was gone. I bolted upright in bed and opened and closed my eyes, again and again. I looked sideways and up and down. It was gone! Completely gone!

I laughed, sobbed, and worshipped all at once as tears ran down my face. Not only had He heard me, but for reasons known only to Him, He also lovingly chose to heal my eye at that moment.

"Oh, Father," I cried, "You are amazing! Thank You! Thank You!"

I was so excited I didn't know what to do first. I called everyone I knew who had been praying for me. Then I rushed to the store and bought the sign. I hung it in my bedroom, so it would be the first thing I would see in the morning when I opened my eyes.

It's still there today. I know other days will come when fear and doubt will show up again and threaten my faith. But this is my constant reminder that my Father gives me His strength when my faith runs weak, and He always hears me. He will always be faithful to me. Not because I deserve His faithfulness, or anything else, because I don't. But because it's who He is— to me, to all who are His.

God Does Not Leave You to Breathe Alone

Lynne Hartke

Without warning, the earth gave way beneath my feet. Tumbling into the hole, the walls of dirt collapsed on top of me as I struggled to stand.

As I screamed for help, falling debris filled my mouth. My nose. My eyes. The more I resisted, the faster the dirt packed around me, crushing my chest.

I COULD NOT BREATHE.

In my fading vision, I saw a man above me, scrambling to rescue me from being buried alive. I extended my one free hand, stretching my fingers as much as possible for him to save me.

Panic filled his face when he could not reach me. He could not help me.

Sucking in one final gasp of air . . . I woke up.

It had been a nightmare. A terrifying, but realistic nightmare.

One problem remained: I still could not breathe.

———•◦•———

I had arrived at our cabin in northern Arizona for a change of scenery after a month-long bout with illness. A simple cold had settled into my chest, resulting in bronchitis and an asthmatic flare. It was my first illness since I had recovered from a 14-month battle with long Covid, a difficult season that had left me with a first-time diagnosis of adult asthma.

The season also left me with a sense of having been betrayed by my own body—and, to be honest, by God, the creator and sustainer of my life. The giver of my breath. If I couldn't trust Him with my breathing, could I trust Him at all? Did He see me? Did He even know me?

> I will be glad and rejoice in your love, for you saw my affliction and knew the anguish of my soul. You have not given me into the hands of the enemy but have set my feet in a spacious place.
>
> —PSALM 31:7–8 (NIV)

The questions increased as I hacked and wheezed for weeks, forcing the cancellation of one engagement after another. I discovered one of the lasting residuals of the pandemic was intolerance for those who were struck by horrible coughing fits in public. Unwilling to be the recipient of the understandable glares of uneasiness and fear from total strangers, I decided to spend a long weekend by myself at our remote cabin. Without the presence of others, I could cough and recover in peace.

After a relaxing day of puttering around the property with our rusty-haired mutt, Mollie, I anticipated a relaxing sleep surrounded by the scent of cedar, pine, and spruce trees.

But then . . . the nightmare.

Still gasping for air, I practiced the breathing techniques I had learned while recovering from long Covid. "Don't panic," I reminded myself. "You've been in this situation before. You know what to do."

Mollie paced around me as I fumbled for my rescue inhaler and tested my oxygen levels. Adrenaline pumped through my veins. And not just adrenaline. Fear.

Panic rose as I rehearsed every worst-case scenario.

Why had I thought that coming to our cabin in the middle of nowhere was a good idea? What will I do if I need to get to the hospital 30 miles away? Will the volunteer fire department arrive in time? What will happen to Mollie?

I checked my oxygen levels again. I was not in the danger zone. My struggle was no longer a physical one.

The darkness of the moonless night crept through the windows of the cabin, reminding me of the nightmare of dirt blocking out the light. Of the fact that I was alone. I switched on a lamp. And another.

The light did not help. Nor did the presence of Mollie nudging my knee with her nose as she sensed my rising anxiety. The *what-if* scenarios continued, no longer focused on my current reality, but a spiraling pit of fear encompassing my past long illness.

What if this flare leads to another 14-month struggle? What if I need to give up hiking again? What if I can't walk Mollie around the block without gasping? What if I need 10 hours of sleep each night and two naps during the day to deal with the fatigue?

What if?

Fear is a terrible tyrant.

Desperate to quiet the noise of impending doom inside my head, I pulled up a sleep meditation app on my phone as I slowed my breath, counting out my inhales and exhales. Scrolling through the options, I clicked on a new meditation from a narrator I had previously enjoyed.

The narrator's soothing voice reminded me to breathe. To relax the tension in my shoulders. In my face. In my hands. To find a comfortable position and prepare for rest. Mollie settled beside me as the voice continued.

> **In his hand is the life of every creature and the breath of all mankind.**
>
> —JOB 12:10 (NIV)

"I will be glad and rejoice in your love," the voice read from Psalm 31:7–8 (NIV), "for you saw my affliction and knew the anguish of my soul. You have not given me into the hands of the enemy but have set my feet in a spacious place."

Hope stirred for the first time since the cough had settled in my chest to rattle my bones. To rattle my faith. I was not handed over to the enemy. God had a spacious place for me. In the pitch blackness of the night, God's truth arrived like a breath of fresh air. I was seen. Known. Not forgotten.

The reassuring voice continued reading scriptures, reminding me of God's presence in times of trouble. The quiet words went on for several minutes, as the Spirit of God brought peace to the room. To my heart.

As the narrator listed ways my Savior was near, he added, "God does not leave you to breathe alone."

I was instantly alert. *What had he said?*

The voice repeated, "God does not leave you to breathe alone."

The pressing anxiety lifted from my shoulders. From my chest. I was not alone. My Jesus, who loves me, spoke through a voice on a sleep app to deliver specific words of comfort to me.

I fell asleep. Not a jittery sleep where every sound woke me up. No. A deep, restorative sleep.

In the morning, I opened my phone to listen to the meditation from the night before. I wanted to take notes and record the experience in my journal.

"That's strange," I said to Mollie, who had jumped up on the couch beside me. "The story I clicked on last night isn't available." In fact, the story was only for paid subscribers, not for those who only had the free version. Like me.

For weeks I had doubted the promises of God were for me, as I viewed life through a narrow slit of scarcity, as narrow as my bronchial tubes on my worst coughing days.

God unlocked the story so I could access the life-giving words when I needed them. He brought me to a spacious place—not only with plenty of breathing room for my lungs, but breathing room for my soul. In a remote cabin, God reached out to remind me that He had not left me alone. Not in the past. Not now. Not in the future.

He was as close as my very breath.

"Hey Mollie," I said, grabbing her leash. "Do you want to go for a long walk?"

The Red Suit Prayer

Lisa Toney

OK, God. I wore my red power suit today. I need to feel strong and confident, because You know that today is the day. I'm unsure what to do here, but I know You do. I believe You have called me to be a part of Your vision for the church. You are calling me to go to seminary to train, think, lead. You have confirmed this to me repeatedly through other people, prayer, and Your Word. Yet my boyfriend does not want me to go. So, I'm going to take a lead from Scripture: "I will place a wool fleece on the threshing floor. If there is dew only on the fleece and all the ground is dry, then I will know that you will save Israel by my hand, as you said" (Judges 6:37, NIV).

I'm going to put a fleece out there. I'm not even sure if I can do that, but I will ask for Your guidance through this.

So here is my fleece. If my work convention gets over early, I'll go straight to my boyfriend's house, knock on the door, break up with him, and go to seminary. If my work conference does not end early, I'll stay and take that as a sign that I should not move forward with all of this. Amen.

———————◆———————

I got out early.

The first thought that went through my mind was, *Oh boy, am I really doing this?*

I must have played that conversation with God over in my head a thousand times. All the way from my booth to the restroom. From the restroom to pack up my booth. From the convention center to my car. From the car to his house. And one more time before I knocked on the door.

I was pretty confident that I had a clear leading from God that it was time to go. It was still hard, though. Someone I cared about had a different opinion, and that made me hesitate.

After all, there were a million reasons to stay. My family was here. My friends were here. My history was here. My boyfriend too. Would God really call me to leave all that and start something new? Was I strong enough? Was I brave enough? Could I really do it?

Eventually I learned those were the wrong questions. I could not do it on my own. But with Jesus, I could. He was strong enough. He was brave enough. He believed I could do it. He called me to do it.

Sensing God's calling for your life can be a challenging process. I talk with many who are living with a lot of uncertainty. For me, it was a gradual move toward being sure of His will.

It started during a time when I was feeling disillusioned. I was frustrated that the church was not more relevant to everyday life struggles. I longed for the joy. Where was the fun? I was not—and am still not—a fan of grumpy Christians whose faces look forever puckered around some sour communion juice they drank a decade ago. Don't get me wrong, there is absolutely a time for mourning, a time for grief, and a time to say that things are not OK. I just get saddened when the joy of the Lord is not present in Church. After all, Jesus came to bring abundant life! The Church is His Bride!

Rather than allowing me to step away, God invited me to step in more fully. The Spirit said to me, "If you don't like what is happening, then go and get trained and *be the change.*"

Sometimes, staying is easier. It is more comfortable. It is familiar. It doesn't require a lot of change. Other times, staying is harder. I have learned to pay attention to the tipping point. Stay until it is harder to stay than it is to go. When the Spirit says it is time, then go.

> **"I will place a wool fleece on the threshing floor. If there is dew only on the fleece and all the ground is dry, then I will know . . ."**
>
> —JUDGES 6:37 (NIV)

My boyfriend had a great job and was a good human. He loved Jesus. But he didn't love the idea of me pursuing leadership within the church. I heard something different from Jesus, though, and Jesus is my first love. So, I made a commitment to Jesus that I would surrender all to Him first.

When I took a deep breath and knocked on my boyfriend's door to have that conversation, it was not easy. The words that came out of my mouth were far from eloquent. I cried. My heart hurt.

Later, it only got worse. I dreaded talking to my friends. They did not want me to go. My family did not want me to go. All. The. Things. But I still knew that it was what I was supposed to do to honor the first love in my life, Jesus.

Truly, *this* is why we have Jesus—for the hard moments of pivotal change. It is at times like these that we realize that we can, and must, lean into His strength to cover over our many weaknesses.

I wore my red power suit and red heels to feel brave. Honestly, they did give a measure of courage. But outer courage will only get you so far. It is the inner courage that drives the day. The courage to lean into the power of Christ is what allows us to do things beyond our confidence level. We trade our limitations for God's limitless power. Transitioning from independence to dependence on God doesn't always feel like a power move. But I've come to see that power moves are less about us and more about obedience. God's mighty hand moves far more effectively than my limited strength. Faith is all about navigating life while yielding to the power moves of the Divine.

God gives courage for hard things. He did for me and He will for you.

His Message on a License Plate

Kathy Glow

As I drove home from the hospital, I gripped the steering wheel, trying to release the tension that had built up over the last several days. I hoped I would be able to sleep once I got home to my own bed after several restless nights in a hospital chair. But as I squinted into the lights of oncoming traffic, the doctor's crushing words kept coming back to me: "Bad news—it's a tumor."

The biopsy, the waiting, and then the final blow: "Your son will die from this."

Joey was just five years old, a vibrant, happy, and precocious child. He was our oldest and most dearly wished-for child, arriving after 14 months of struggling with infertility and praying that our dreams of parenthood would come true. Always busy, always thinking of new things to do and learn, Joey had been having debilitating headaches followed by bouts of vomiting. Then one day, he suffered a grand mal seizure.

I was utterly shocked and dismayed. I didn't understand what was happening or why. How could God, who was supposed to love us, cause a five-year-old child so much pain? Were we, his parents, being punished for something? I didn't know what to do. Prayers were failing me, so I turned to social media. I wrote posts on Facebook and started an online journal. Maybe other people's prayers and support would help.

However, much of their support came in the form of, "We will pray for a miracle!" and "We will pray for healing!" and "I read about someone with this same tumor, and he was miraculously healed! Joey will be, too!"

I am married to a surgeon, who spent nights researching for something that could cure our son. He was looking for a percentage, a number, a study that would give hope. But there were none.

I didn't understand why this beautiful, happy little boy had to suffer and be taken away from us. No prayer or miracle was going to save him. Despite being a lifelong Catholic, I became angry with God.

That night, driving home from the hospital, I pulled up behind a car at a stoplight. Its license plate read: "He Heals."

I was just blocks away from our house. I hadn't ever seen this car, so I was sure that this was a message meant for me. But what could it possibly mean? Joey was going to die. I could feel a rage bubbling over inside me that I hadn't yet set free. I began yelling at the back of the car from inside of mine.

"He heals?! That's crap! He's never going to heal Joey. There is no miracle. He will never be healed!" Although no one could hear me, it felt good to openly deny the God that the person in the car in front of me espoused. I just kept thinking, *Why won't he ever be healed, God? Why not?*

Throughout his illness, our church pastor, Father Dan, had visited Joey in the hospital. I had tensed the first time I saw him, thinking he would explain Joey's cancer away with a Bible verse. Instead, he prayed with me, hugged me, and told me he didn't have any answers. I was still thinking about that license plate when he next visited, so I cautiously told him about it. He wasn't sure what to make of it either, simply saying, "Hmm, that's interesting. You may have to wait for the meaning to be revealed."

As Joey grew sicker and weaker over the following months, I often thought about that license plate message. Every time I thought about it, those angry and bitter feelings emerged again. Our son wasn't being healed. We were planning his funeral. I constantly imagined what it would be like to say goodbye to and then bury my child. Each time I tried to pray, I stopped. I felt defeated, betrayed.

> **This is the confidence we have in approaching God: that if we ask anything according to his will, he hears us.**
>
> —1 JOHN 5:14 (NIV)

Joey died almost 14 months after his initial diagnosis. He was just six-and-a-half years old. The only "healing" came in the form of his death, an end to his suffering and our family's nightmare.

That summer, I struggled to get out of bed each morning. I felt helpless and hopeless. I had Joey's three younger siblings to care for, though, so I slowly trudged forward, searching for my own healing, still angry with God. I worked hard that summer and fall to find joy in the activities that we had always loved as a family. Harder still was wrapping my mind around being a mom to three sons and not four.

One day that fall, I took a pregnancy test. It was unexpectedly positive. I didn't want another baby. I had turned 40 years old the month before Joey died, my self-appointed baby cutoff age. I had given all my baby items and maternity clothes away, thinking that it was too late to use them again.

As the baby grew inside me, I convinced myself that something would be terribly wrong with them. After all, God had betrayed me once. I was betting He'd do it again.

"There has to be something wrong," I would say to my doctor at every appointment. Despite my insistence, she kept reassuring me the baby was growing normally. I didn't want to look at any of the ultrasounds. I didn't want to see it or fall in love again. It was just too painful.

At the 20-week ultrasound, we found out it would be another boy. I felt sad and angry and duped. I didn't want a replacement son. I wanted the one I had before.

> **Seek the LORD and his strength; seek his presence continually.**
>
> —1 CHRONICLES 16:11 (NRSVUE)

The rest of my pregnancy progressed with doubt and fear as I tried to push any feelings of excitement deep down in a place I couldn't access. It was my way of protecting my heart and getting a leg up on any plans God would have for this baby.

Soon the day arrived when the doctors planned to induce labor, and I gave birth to a beautiful son. The moment he was placed in my arms, he looked up at me with his wide, blue eyes, something that none of my other sons had done—except Joey. Everything washed away: the fear, the doubt, the anger, and much of the sadness. In that moment, I forgot about being mad at God.

We gave our baby his brother's name for a middle name and watched as he learned to hold his head up and smile at the three older brothers who were so in love with him. They read him books and gave him toys and wanted to hold and feed him. Much of the happiness returned in our house, and I began to tell the boys stories about their oldest brother, especially how he always loved to help with each new baby brother who arrived on the scene.

I felt a contentment that had been absent for almost 2 years. As I looked into my baby's eyes, my heart felt at peace. He was so wide-eyed and observant, just as Joey had been as a baby. He even had some of the same mannerisms Joey had. Sometimes during late-night nursing sessions, I would whisper, "Joey, is that you?" I knew it was impossible that God had sent Joey back to me. Yet I felt a similarity between the two boys that I couldn't deny.

> **The LORD is near to all who call on him, to all who call on him in truth.**
>
> —PSALMS 145:18 (NIV)

One Sunday, as we were leaving Mass, I saw Father Dan, the same pastor who had pondered the meaning of "He Heals" with me. Suddenly, a realization hit me like a lightning bolt: the healing message hadn't been about Joey. It had been about me. It was about me learning to love again. It was for me to open my heart and recognize that life could go on even after the death of my child. It was for me to realize that God had never planned on punishing me or abandoning me. He wanted me to know that He would always be right there beside me in grief and in joy.

I shared my revelation with Father Dan, and he smiled gently. "God is certainly great, isn't He?"

In the years since Joey's death, I have had to heal my fractured relationship with God. I've pondered the meaning of the

"He heals" message many times. Though I'll carry the scars of my grief with me forever, I'm able to laugh with my sons and share stories of their brother. And when the youngest, who never even met Joey, tells the perfect "Joey" story, that's when those two words that once enraged me finally ring true.

He heals.

While it wasn't the message I wanted, it was the one He knew I needed.

When the Student Is Ready

Roberta Messner

I trudged into my new physician's office, the hopelessness in my spirit heavier than the pounds I carried. "I've piled on over a hundred pounds," I wailed. "Honestly! I eat next to nothing." I watched his eyes for any sign of contempt, for proof he didn't believe me. There was only kindness.

"I've seen this over and over," he said. "The meds you've taken have messed with your metabolism. It's virtually impossible to reverse it, especially as we age." He added, "You're now in excellent health, but that's going to change if you don't lose weight."

I was tired of it all. The empty promises. The humiliation. The hopelessness that moves in when you believe your situation can never change. There was no place to hide the pain and shame. I might as well post my picture on a billboard: *Undisciplined. Lazy. Doesn't care about herself. You probably wouldn't like her.*

Outside the office, I tilted my head up to the heavens and prayed. Surely the Creator of the universe knew a solution to my dilemma.

A few days later, I was in the parking lot of a large chain store sipping an ice-cold cherry cola—my one comfort in this world—when a fellow in high-bib overalls ambled over. He was peddling a brown grocery sack with a head of broccoli hanging out the top. He spoke with a heavy accent that I didn't recognize, praising the health benefits of vegetables and berries with antioxidant properties.

Lord, have mercy. This wasn't what I'd prayed for.

"If you'd trade those 17 teaspoons of sugar you're drinking for my produce, you'd get better," he said. The nerve. Who told him something was wrong with me? He grinned toward the black hand-lettering on his dented tan truck. "FOOD'LL FIX YOU!"

I was having none of it. I declined his produce and walked away.

Since starving myself wasn't working, I signed up for physical therapy. While exercising, I pulled a muscle, and something new hurt. I popped a few over-the-counter analgesics and ended up in kidney failure. My body swelled. My blood pressure shot up. Nausea and vomiting led to dehydration, which caused my joints to scream in pain.

A project deadline was past due. I'd asked for several extensions, but my day of reckoning came. I sequestered myself at the back table at a local coffee shop and vowed to get it done.

A fellow nurse I didn't know slid into the seat across from me and struck up a conversation. "You look familiar," she said. "I used to work Surgery at St. Mary's." Out of the blue she told of a surgeon she'd once known who spoke kindly to her patients—even to their organs—as she operated. But the doctor was now into *preventing* disease. "She cares for the whole patient so they can be their healthiest."

"Well, sign me up!" I said. "I've tried everything else."

I called the doctor's office, and within 5 minutes was telling my life story to the doctor's receptionist. "I'm having joint pain beyond belief," I said. "And there's something no one can figure out. After years of taking medications, I cannot take off the weight I've gained."

"We see that all the time," the receptionist assured me. "I believe she can help you."

The doctor was booked up for four months, but her office mailed me a dietary packet. I scanned the pages of instructions.

> **I will instruct you and teach you in the way you should go.**
>
> **—PSALM 32:8 (NIV)**

No refined sugar. No bread, red meat, or processed foods. Instead, fruits, vegetables, protein, and Omega-3 fatty acids. If I couldn't fish it, dig it out of the ground, or yank it off a bush, I couldn't have it.

Pain or no pain, weight or no weight, this was impossible. I didn't even *like* those foods, much less believe they could help me. The bulging envelope went straight to my junk drawer.

But I couldn't sleep or move without pain. *If you don't do something, you're going to be an invalid, Roberta.* One morning I reached into my junk drawer and actually read those instructions.

It was called an anti-inflammatory diet. When I Googled it, I learned that the root cause of many chronic diseases is inflammation, often brought on by what we eat. It seemed ridiculous until I remembered a friend who'd followed a similar regimen when he was diagnosed with cancer. When he went into remission, his doctor said his diet had been as important as the chemo.

Armed with the packet, I was at my usual grocery store when the doors opened. A lady with a name tag that said Gina was putting out produce. Seeing the befuddled look on my face, she offered to help. "The strawberries and blueberries are as sweet as sugar today," she said. That sounded promising, seeing as refined sugar topped the No list. "You'll learn to love green tea. Now, you'll want to get a plant-based sweetener. Walnuts and salmon for those Omega-3s."

I'd shopped at this grocery store for years, but I'd never had a tour guide. Whenever I thought of cheating and snagging an ice-cold cherry cola, Gina's face would appear in my mind. She'd seemed so sure I could do it. I returned a few days later to stock up on berries and those good collard greens and broccoli she convinced me to try. "I'm looking for Gina," I told another worker. "My joint pain's nearly gone since she helped me with more healthy eating."

"Gina? *Gina?*" she said, shaking her head. "Gina lives on Monster drinks and Cheetos."

> # I would not obey my teachers or turn my ear to my instructors.
>
> **—PROVERBS 5:13 (NIV)**

The day of my appointment with my new doctor finally arrived. With pain in the past, I was sleeping through the night for the first time in memory. Doing things around my cabin and even exercising. When the nurse weighed me, I was stunned to see I'd dropped 31 pounds.

My new doctor was as excited about my turnaround as I was. And she believed in me. Best of all, I was beginning to believe in me too. "I need some more labs, but this seems to point to a problem called leptin miscommunication," she said. She explained it was a fairly recent discovery, how leptin is a metabolic hormone, and when it's out of balance, your body holds onto fat for dear life no matter how much you cut back on eating.

She leaned her head in my direction and smiled. "It's hard for folks to believe this, Roberta. Food will fix you. You're proof of that."

Her words took me back to the farmer in the parking lot. God had answered my prayer after all, in a subtly simple way. And then when I didn't listen the first time, He sent a nurse to connect me with a doctor who could lead me to the right diet.

> **Although the Lord gives you the bread of adversity and the water of affliction, your teachers will be hidden no more; with your own eyes you will see them.**
>
> —ISAIAH 30:20 (NIV)

I no longer have cravings for the cherry cola that sabotaged me. In fact, I hardly think about food at all. The whole approach has become a way of life. My metabolism has tripled, and in 2 years, I've lost 133 pounds. For 5 of those months, my mobility was limited from an injury, yet I never regained an ounce. I underwent three big surgeries with completely normal labs, on no medications, and with no other health issues. My new lifestyle had prepared me for a better surgical outcome and rehabilitation.

Years of surgeries, procedures, and medications all had their place. But in the despair of chronic illness and pain, I'd overlooked my own power to alter my lifestyle.

My doctor's approach to care is highly personalized. It's the same with God. He knew my penchant for serendipity—and, yes, the absurd. He charmed and coaxed me with an unlikely

GOD'S GIFT OF TASTE
— Lynne Hartke —

HAVE YOU EVER eaten dandelion greens? Compared in flavor to kale or arugula, they are rich in vitamin A, iron, and calcium. The scientific name is *Taraxacum officinale*. The first part of the name comes from the Greek word *taraxos*, meaning "disorder," and *akos*, meaning "remedy." The second part, the species name, meant that at one time dandelions were on the official list from which physicians could write prescriptions. Believed to have strong medicinal properties, people throughout the centuries have used dandelions for various ailments. In Genesis 1:11–12, God called His created plants and vegetation "good," including the lowly dandelion.

cast of characters who pointed the way. It all began with a farmer in a parking lot, getting the student ready for when her teacher would take center stage.

The Lord's Sense of Humor

Renee Yancy

I've always loved playing practical jokes. I have some seriously clever pranks to my credit, including fake birthday cakes made out of Styrofoam and turning a conservative friend's front yard into a gaudy Christmas wonderland. But there was one time that the Lord proved to me that He has a sense of humor too.

This particular incident in my life took place when I was a young woman attending the Christian Center Church in Brockport, New York, where I first heard the Gospel and became born again.

I was single. An attractive, divorced man with four little children wanted me to be his wife. He was an accomplished musician who served on the worship team, and his attention flattered me, but deep in my heart I knew this relationship wasn't meant to be.

I had been a Christian for about 2 years at that time, and I was still in the process of learning to hear the Lord's voice. Slowly, I realized that the Holy Spirit was urging me to break it off with this man. But I wasn't ready to do it. I had questions. Was it really the Lord's voice I was hearing?

My old pastor, Don Riling, used to say, "Make it easy on yourself and tough on God." The first time I heard that from him, I didn't know what to think. It seemed disrespectful. What I came to understand was that he meant God can handle it. He knows everything about us; nothing is hidden from Him. He knows exactly where we live and how to get to us!

With Pastor Don's words firmly in mind, I decided that if the Lord wanted me to break up with this man, I would make it tough on Him—and I had the perfect opportunity coming up. My church had scheduled a day conference on motivational gifts with a popular and charismatic teacher by the name of Marilyn Hickey. The venue was a Holiday Inn in Batavia, New York.

At that time, I served in the sound ministry—setting up microphones and electrical cords, running the sound checks for church services and events, and so on. I was to assist with the conference at the hotel. I told the Lord I would ask Marilyn Hickey what she thought about my situation. And whatever she told me to do, I would do and receive it as coming from the Lord.

> **"God has brought me laughter, and everyone who hears about this will laugh with me."**
>
> **—GENESIS 21:6 (NIV)**

But then I arranged the "tough" part: I stayed as far away from Marilyn Hickey as I could get. If I saw her anywhere near me, I would quickly move away. Marilyn cut a striking figure, tall with a confident air about her, so she was easy to spot.

I was as drawn in by her teachings as everyone else. Dressed fashionably in a tailored suit and wearing brown-and-white leather spectator pumps, she delivered a fascinating teaching on motivational gifts from Romans 12:6–8 (NIV): *If your gift is prophesying, then prophesy in accordance with your faith; if it is serving, then serve; if it is teaching, then teach; if it is to encourage, then give encouragement; if it is giving, then give generously; if it is to lead, do it diligently; if it is to show mercy, do it cheerfully.*

She used the image of a spilled and broken glass of water to illustrate the seven motivational gifts. If someone had the gift of giving, that person responded by buying a new glass to replace the broken one. If it was teaching, that person would instruct the person who spilled the water how to avoid doing it again. The person with the motivational gift of serving would get a fresh glass of water, and so on.

A time to weep and a time to laugh.

—ECCLESIASTES 3:4 (NIV)

It was a day-long conference with coffee breaks and workshops, and I managed to avoid Marilyn the entire 10 hours we were there.

The conference ended late in the afternoon. People hung out for a while in conversation and discussion and then went home. The conference room emptied, and Marilyn Hickey left. We broke down all the equipment, packed the church van, and were ready to leave. Rather smugly, I congratulated myself on having successfully managed to never give Marilyn the chance to speak to me.

I needed to make a quick stop in the restroom before we started the 24-mile trip back home. I noticed that the ladies' room was completely empty when I went into a stall. After a moment, the door opened. The tap, tap, tap of high heels on the tile floor echoed through the room. Someone entered the stall next to mine. I glanced down at the shoes that showed below the adjoining wall.

White-and-brown leather spectator pumps.

Just like the ones Marilyn Hickey had worn today.

I closed my eyes and groaned internally. I wasn't so smart after all.

I could have waited for her to leave, but I *knew* the Lord had arranged this—exactly as I had challenged Him to.

I left the safety of my stall as Ms. Hickey washed her hands at the sink. I approached her, my heart pounding in my chest. She turned and gave me an inquiring glance.

I could barely get the words out. "I have to ask you a question," I said. She nodded graciously. I proceeded to give her a quick synopsis of my situation and told her that I would receive her counsel as coming from the Lord.

"Slice it." Two words. She spoke them with authority and decisiveness. I can still remember that moment, clear as day. I think I felt a bit shell-shocked at how the Lord had arranged the entire scenario. In the bathroom, for heaven's sake.

But I knew that the Lord had definitely spoken to me. And I obeyed. I broke the relationship off and moved on. And a year later, the Lord brought the man who was to be my husband into my life. Forty-five years later, we are still growing in the Lord together.

The Lord can always find a way to speak to us—and sometimes in creative, personal ways. In this case, knowing my love for practical jokes, He played one on me. Even though it had a serious message, He had to have been chuckling as He perfectly arranged to deliver the message!

We can trust that He knows what He's doing. And we can be sure that He desires to speak to us and direct us, and that He has a plan for our lives.

All these years later, I still smile when I remember how He got me. Whew. I'm sure glad I listened!

Stepping Stones

Dorci Harris

I'd walked into a church one Sunday morning, and my life changed. I'd believed in Jesus since I was a child, but it was that day that the Lord met me, filling me with His Holy Spirit. Suddenly, everything looked brand-new.

Ten years later, my journey with the Lord still felt as if it had just begun. I was slowly learning how to trust Him, how to walk in this new kind of life. He had led me to become a stay-at-home mom to our two sons—a challenge, even if it was a fun one—and He'd always provided for our little family. But it took a very special series of events to show me just how much I could trust Him.

Having my boys was a dream, but there were moments I needed to escape to a little peace and quiet. One time, while out driving at night, I found just the place. On the outskirts of town, about 10 miles from home, there was a secluded street with just a few homes that gave way to an unpaved road. There was a stop sign where it crossed another road—Happy Valley, according to the street sign—and then the unlit dirt road continued into a quiet desert full of cacti, tumbleweeds, and palo verde trees. Mountains rose up from all sides, and every now and then the sounds of howling coyotes in the distance pierced the darkness. I came to love this peaceful road, and every now and then, I'd take a break to drive through it and absorb its beauty.

As time passed, our tiny starter home seemed to be getting smaller all the time, and we decided to look for something a little bit bigger. We walked through a few houses for sale, but nothing seemed right. We kept praying the Lord would lead us, and we asked our friends to pray too. It was going to take a tiny miracle to find something big enough for growing boys, yet affordable for our one-income family.

One day I took a break and drove down my favorite road. I stopped at the stop sign, though I had never seen anyone else on the crossroad. Just past the intersection there was a large trailer on an empty piece of land on one side of the road and a sign indicating that there would be new homes under construction.

Huh. That's interesting.

I didn't let myself get my hopes up, but I couldn't wait to drive down my road again soon. When I did, I saw the model homes being built. My husband and I talked about it, and thought we'd go visit just for the fun of it.

We walked through the model homes and found one that seemed perfect. It wasn't fancy—it was the smallest one—but it was still almost twice the size of where we'd been living. *Do we dare? How could we, though?*

We went home and crunched the numbers. We prayed about it. Our friends prayed about it. Finances would be tight, but we soon found ourselves back in the builder's office. We looked at the available lots, and though we loved one that was in a quiet cul-de-sac, the cost of that lot was a slightly higher premium. We chose a lot in another area, one that was on an entry street into the neighborhood, and gave them our down payment.

That lot on the corner of the cul-de-sac wouldn't leave my mind, though, so I prayed some more. Soon we were back in the office changing our lot to the one in the cul-de-sac, where our boys could grow up in the quiet and safety of this tucked-away area.

We couldn't believe what God was doing for us. He'd led me down a road I came to love, all along knowing He had a plan for our growing family, a plan far more than we ever could have expected.

We sold our first house and moved into an apartment while waiting for our new home to be built. We were on our way.

Soon afterward, my husband told me there were rumors of layoffs going around among the employees. *Surely God won't let him be laid off now.* I told him, though, if he was laid off to call and let me know before he came home. I'd need a few moments to process.

> **For in the gospel God's righteousness is being revealed from faith to faith, as it is written, "The righteous will live by faith."**
>
> —ROMANS 1:17 (ISV)

Soon afterward, the phone rang. "I'm coming home."

Of course, this was no surprise to God. In the place of anxiety about money and our impending new home purchase, He filled me with a strength of faith I'd never known before. We started praying again. Our friends started praying again.

Before long, to our great relief, my husband found a new job that paid slightly more than the last one. For a couple of weeks we relaxed, thinking God's plan was now complete.

Then he was laid off again. He started the job-hunting process all over.

Our faithful friends continued to pray for us. One day a dear friend came and told me what God had impressed on her heart about my husband's job situation: "The Lord is going to take him from stepping stone to stepping stone until He has him where He wants him to be."

I continued to be filled with an unshakable faith that the Lord was with us, even though it felt as if we were walking out into that desert with no idea where we were going. If we backed out of buying the house now, we'd lose our deposit. If we went ahead, though, would my husband have a job? If he found a job, would it pay enough?

The builders framed the house and my husband kept looking for another job. He soon found one, and again, this job paid a little more than the last one.

The walls went up, and, like clockwork, he was laid off again. This same process continued another time or two, each succeeding job with a slight bump in pay. Stepping stone to stepping stone.

> **We all, with unveiled faces, are looking as in a mirror at the glory of the Lord and are being transformed into the same image from glory to glory; this is from the Lord who is the Spirit.**
>
> —2 CORINTHIANS 3:18 (CSB)

By the time we walked through our nearly completed home, the Lord had taken my husband to the last stepping stone, a job he's had now for more than 20 years.

My trust in the Lord had grown, too, from stepping stone to stepping stone, from faith to faith. With each new step as I walked with God, He continued to slough off the disillusionment from my previous life without Him, giving me a brand-new sense of my identity in Him. I was no longer the person I had been. He was my faithful Father, and I was His daughter.

Just before my family moved into our new house, the Lord spoke to my heart once more, this time using words from thousands of years before:

> For the LORD your God is bringing you into a good land of flowing streams and pools of water, with fountains and springs that gush out in the valleys and hills. . . . It is a land where food is plentiful and nothing is lacking. . . . When you have eaten your fill, be sure to praise the LORD your God for the good land he has given you. (Deuteronomy 8:7, 9, 10, NLT)

Our Heavenly Father did indeed bring us into a "Happy Valley," a place where we always had what we needed. A number of years later, He even graciously provided us with the "pool of water."

In the many years since, we have never forgotten His goodness and that He is the one who provided and continues to provide everything we have, and we praise His name.

Contributors

Acknowledgments

Every attempt has been made to credit the sources of copyrighted material used in this book. If any such acknowledgment has been inadvertently omitted or miscredited, receipt of such information would be appreciated.

"Blessed Assurance" lyrics by Fanny J. Crosby, 1873.

Scripture quotations marked (CSB) are taken from *The Christian Standard Bible*, copyright © 2017 by Holman Bible Publishers. Used by permission.

Scripture quotations marked (ESV) are taken from *The Holy Bible, English Standard Version*. Copyright © 2001 by Crossway Bibles, a division of Good News Publishers. Used by permission. All rights reserved.

Scripture quotations marked (ISV) are taken from the *International Standard Version*. Copyright © 1995–2014 by ISV Foundation. All rights reserved internationally. Used by permission of Davidson Press, LLC.

Scripture quotations marked (KJV) are taken from the *King James Version of the Bible*.

Scripture quotations marked (NASB) are taken from the *New American Standard Bible*®, Copyright © 1960, 1971, 1977, 1995, 2020 by The Lockman Foundation. All rights reserved.

Scripture quotations marked (NIV) are taken from *The Holy Bible, New International Version*®, *NIV*®. Copyright © 1973, 1978, 1984, 2011 by Biblica, Inc. Used by permission. All rights reserved worldwide.

Scripture quotations marked (NKJV) are taken from the *New King James Version*®. Copyright © 1982 by Thomas Nelson. Used by permission. All rights reserved.

Scripture quotations marked (NLT) are taken from the *Holy Bible, New Living Translation*. Copyright © 1996, 2004, 2007, 2015 by Tyndale House Foundation. Used by permission of Tyndale House Publishers Inc., Carol Stream, Illinois. All rights reserved.

Scripture quotations marked (NRSVUE) are taken from the *New Revised Standard Version, Updated Edition*. Copyright © 2021 National Council of Churches of Christ in the United States of America. Used by permission. All rights reserved worldwide.

Scripture quotations marked (RSV) are taken from the *Revised Standard Version of the Bible*. Copyright © 1946, 1952, 1971 by the Division of Christian Education of the National Council of the Churches of Christ in the United States of America. Used by permission.

A Note from the Editors

We hope you enjoyed *Lifted by His Word*, published by Guideposts. For more than 75 years, Guideposts, a nonprofit organization, has been driven by a vision of a world filled with hope. We aspire to be the voice of a trusted friend, a friend who makes you feel more hopeful and connected.

By making a purchase from Guideposts, you join our community in touching millions of lives, inspiring them to believe that all things are possible through faith, hope, and prayer. Your continued support allows us to provide uplifting resources to those in need. Whether through our communities, websites, apps, or publications, we inspire our audiences, bring them together, and comfort, uplift, entertain, and guide them. Visit us at guideposts.org to learn more.

We would love to hear from you. Write us at Guideposts, P.O. Box 5815, Harlan, Iowa 51593 or call us at (800) 932-2145. Did you love *Lifted by His Word?* Leave a review for this product on guideposts.org/shop. Your feedback helps others in our community find relevant products.

Find inspiration, find faith, find Guideposts.
Shop our best sellers and favorites at
guideposts.org/shop

Or scan the QR code to go directly to our Shop

Printed in the United States
by Baker & Taylor Publisher Services